ISBN: 978-0-9829868-0-6

Published by R+S Media, San Francisco, California

Quote by David Sylvian courtesy Innerviews.org and Anil Prasad.

Should I Go To Law School?

The $100,000 Gamble

Derek S. Roberti, PhD, JD

"We need to go the other way to find and create work that is provocative and can steal up on us where we're relatively unaware and really blow our hearts and minds wide open."

David Sylvian

CONTENTS

INTRODUCTION

THE $100,000 GAMBLE

What makes law school a gamble? For most people, gambling isn't the first thing that comes to mind when they think of going to law school. People think of law school as an academic decision, a career move or maybe just an easy answer to the "What should I do with my life?" question.

Often people are aware of the cultural mythology about lawyers: they work long hours, under combative conditions and are often profoundly unsatisfied with their lives. Or they may traffic in other stereotypes: between driving their Ferraris and being fitted for yet another Armani suit, lawyers make moving orations in front of spellbound juries. While neither of these clichés give you much to go on when considering law school, many prospective students begin the application process without knowing much more than this.

That's what I call a gamble.

There are several characteristics that define a gamble:

Every gamble has stakes. For the law school decision, the stakes are, on average, $80,000 in law school debt and at least another $60,000 in lost income during the three years of law school. But much more important than the financial stakes are the personal stakes. Most law school applicants don't dig deeply into the lifestyle of attorneys and don't understand the lived experience of what it's like to be a lawyer – both the good and the bad.

Gambling has odds. In law, the odds are determined by your LSAT score, your undergraduate GPA and the school you get accepted to. If you are on the high end of all of these measures, you've eliminated a lot of risk from the wager. But, even then, a rocky economy throws much of the predictability of legal status out the window.

Gambling involves luck. This is as true for law school as it is for any other career path in life. What makes legal careers different is that they require dramatically more risk than most other careers. Few other professions require so much of an up-front investment for such an uncertain outcome.

Good gamblers, however, try to improve their odds. They hope to wager as little as possible for as large a payout as possible. To do this, they need information that clarifies the stakes and reduces the role of chance.

If you are considering law school – perhaps thinking of it as a safe career, a well-trodden path to an almost certain job offer – it's time to reframe the question. First off, deciding to go to law school is a risky proposition. It's a *good* proposition for many; but, for others, it just leaves them with a mountain of debt and a feeling of indentured servitude. Second, there are ways to minimize this risk. Gathering information on the financial investment you are making, the lived experience of working attorneys and your own desires and aptitudes is key to clarifying your decision.

Finally, it's important to turn the tables on law school. Because law school has such an elaborate admissions process, it's easy to forget that law school and the legal profession need to prove their worth to you. In other words, rather than just taking the stereotypes of lawyers for granted, you need to understand what you want in a career and make sure that the legal profession can offer you that unlike any other profession. Trying to discern whether you will be a happy, fulfilled lawyer is an essential part of reducing the risk in your law school decision.

When you get clear on the law school decision, your choice changes from a gamble to a well-informed, if not riskless, voyage down a path that allows you to express your life uniquely. The challenge is that most of us don't have a framework for turning a $100,000 gamble into a smart investment. How do you make such a momentous decision?

YOUR DECISION, YOUR LIFE

There are three kinds of people who seriously spend time considering whether or not to apply to law school:

First, there are those who genuinely don't know enough about law school or legal practice to make an informed decision. They ask themselves questions like: "What do you study in law school? What do attorneys do? What are different legal career paths? How much money do lawyers make?"

Second, there are those who have the raw data they need, but are undecided as to whether legal practice is a good fit for their interests and personality.

Finally, there are those who – if they are completely honest with themselves – have all the information they need, but simply aren't 100% satisfied with the conclusion they have reached. This latter group actually knows that they should or should not attend law school, that the thought of legal practice genuinely thrills or repels them; but something is keeping them from accepting the conclusion that they – consciously or unconsciously – have reached.

Whichever group you are in (and maybe you are a little bit in all three), help is on the way. The goal of this book is to provide practical, nuts-and-bolts information and tools to help you make a decision. But I also want to provide you with more than just data and heuristics; I want you to feel confident that your choice makes complete sense to both your mind and your heart.

For those of you who are impatient, there are some shortcuts through this book that will help you find the exact information you are looking for. I'll talk more about that at the end of this Introduction. For now, I hope you'll take a few moments for me to make my case that your deliberation about whether or not to attend law school is far more significant than you may imagine, and it is a decision that deserves your time.

If you have not already been accepted to law school, you have a long and interesting road ahead of you. You will spend many hours studying for your LSAT, taking practice tests, completing applications, writing essays, getting letters of recommendations, assembling copies of your transcripts and writing checks for your application fees. Whether you have started down this path or not, you owe it to yourself to take some time to think clearly, but also deeply, about this moment in your life's journey. It is a moment that will quite literally shape your future and – even if you are 98% sure of your decision already – it should be examined and savored.

There are some obvious things that are unique about this moment in your life and the decision you are making. At the very least, you are deciding how and where to spend three years of your life. Law school will thrill you, it will bore you, it will excite you, and it will profoundly impact any kind of social life you currently experience. If you choose a law school that is located outside your current geographical area, you will leave many of your friends and familiar surroundings and make your new home in a completely different climate, culture and housing situation. Your ultimate path will determine your social relationships for the next three years and for many years to come. You are deciding how you will spend your days working after you graduate from law school and the nature of that work. And, perhaps most obviously, you are making a decision about taking on a significant financial burden with the hope of future financial reward. (Understanding the nature of your financial decision will be part of our work together.)

There are even more significant consequences to your decision that may be less obvious. I am not at all exaggerating when I say that your attendance at law school for three years will change your thinking profoundly. It is a cliché to say that the fundamental goal of law school is to teach you to think like a lawyer. But, for many, law school's impact goes much further. In addition to adding a new set of analytic and argumentative skills to your problem-solving repertoire, thinking like a lawyer may affect how you relate to other people, how you weigh your life decisions and how (or whether) you connect to and express your wholeness as a person.

As a law student, you may find it difficult to relate to your non-law school friends in ways that you once found comfortable and rewarding. You will focus your schedule on law-school activities – studying for class, preparing for exams, participating in student organizations, working for Law Review, competing in Moot Court, etc. Non-law school friends may seem like a nuisance or a distraction in comparison to the pressing and urgent demands of your legal studies. You might think – "I will always be me and my friends will always be my friends" – and you may be right. But even the best relationships will feel the strain of law school if only because there are a finite number of hours in the day. I should also mention that there will be people waiting for you in law school who will blow your mind with their intelligence, friendliness, and generosity. I don't want to suggest that law school will make you lose all of your friends; rather, it will change you, meaning it will change who you relate to, how you relate to them and what you value in your relationships.

While it might seem that legal thinking will make you a smarter, shrewder decision-maker when facing life's vicissitudes, the larger impact on your decision-making process will be legal culture. In law school, you will be surrounded by people who are conservative in how they make decisions. By "conservative," I'm not talking politics; I'm talking about their relationship to risk-taking. It is fair to say that there is much more risk-aversion and much less risk-taking in legal culture. This affects law students in their decisions of which firms to work at, what career paths to explore, and what student activities to participate in (and which ones to eschew). In a sense (at least a self-perpetuating sense), there is good reason for this. Law firms like simple hiring decisions and the vast majority of firms would rather hire someone who was an undergraduate at Harvard and on Law Review at Stanford than someone who took time off after their undergraduate degree at a state university to gain work experience, start a family, pursue a music career, etc. Law firms don't like surprises, so law students tend to conform to certain mores that improve their chances of seeming like an impressive and safe hire. (Note that even if you don't intend to work at a law firm, you will assuredly feel the effect of legal culture on your actions and on everyone around you at law school.)

Legal culture and its conservative mindset profoundly affect practicing lawyers in their life and career decisions. If you speak to a dozen attorneys, you will likely find that at least half of them feel "trapped" in their careers. "Trapped" typically means "afraid to make a change." This feeling of being trapped and without options persists even when the pain experienced in their day-to-day work life is very high. Immersed in legal culture, attorneys primarily know other attorneys who conform to the standards of legal practice and attitudes. If you dare to think outside of the norm – in pursuing a new career, for example – you may feel immobilized, without

...thinking like a lawyer will affect how you relate to other people, how you weigh your life decisions and how (or whether) you connect to and express your wholeness as a person.

options and with very few peers who can practically help you move down a different path. It's not that you will be working with mindless automatons; rather, your peers will be other attorneys who have followed the path laid out for them and who have little experience maneuvering outside that path.

One more note about law school is how it relates to your sense of wholeness as a person. Now, this might seem like an intangible quality or it might even feel irrelevant to you. I mean it here in a very specific way: You are a vastly capable person with many dimensions to your personality and life experience. You may have academic aptitudes, athletic skills, spiritual interests, and even if none of these apply to you, you have a heart, a personality and your own unique way of expressing yourself and connecting with others. It may feel to you like law school is indifferent to these personality attributes and instead is primarily interested in a few small slices of what makes you *you*. Specifically, law school rewards your analytic abilities, your ability to digest very large amounts of material, and your ability to endure long periods of effort without obvious rewards.

It's like you are training to be a body builder, but have an extremely limited variety of exercises that you perform. So, you strengthen your right bicep by doing many curls with increasing amounts of weight; you strengthen your left quadriceps by doing thousands of one-legged squat thrusts; and you strengthen your upper-abdominals just doing stomach crunches. The end result is that you are incredibly developed in some areas of your body, and puny and neglected in other areas of your body. You look great from certain angles, but it's really hard to find clothes that fit.

Law school is like this in that it works very specific areas of your mind and your emotions. You will become an even smarter cookie than you already are and you will have a tremendous ability to delay gratification. Both of these are useful skills in work and in life. If you excel at them, you will excel in the legal profession. But you are so, *so* much more than this. It's not that law school requires that you be a specific type of person; but, practically speaking, you will have to make trade-offs with your time. Holding on to a balanced personality that truly expresses all of your capacities is almost impossible in law school. There are parts of you that will go into hiding during law school and it is up to you to keep remembering that they exist.

Now, all of this may sound somewhat on the negative side; but I want to emphasize that it's not. It is very possible that you will go to law school and make meaningful, lifelong friendships; you will stretch the limits of your analytic horsepower; and you will continue on to a career that endlessly delights and enriches you. This is, in fact, a likely outcome if you are committed to it.

Realistically, your legal training will provide you with both desirable and undesirable experiences. In any case, I promise you that the outcomes will be profound. And this is why I believe that the decision to go to law school or not is much more than an analysis of raw data. This is an incredible moment in your life where you are genuinely giving yourself the opportunity to significantly reshape *who* and *how* you are as a person. As you make your way through this book, I suggest you read it and let your mind wander. Treat your decision with the significance it deserves and don't be afraid to explore all of the consequences and nuances of your choice as they permeate every aspect of your life. Lest you think this is a recipe for indecision, I promise you that it is not. If you read this book from start to finish, you will have concrete answers and a strong sense of confidence about your decision.

I care deeply about your law school decision and I care even more about this moment you are at in your life, where you are taking the courageous act of considering your life's direction. Ninety-five percent of people move through their lives without thinking through life's most important decisions. This puts you in that rare five percent of people who are – through their conscious choices – truly in the driver's seat of their lives. I believe that everyone deserves to express their lives fully, to communicate their memories and their feelings, to connect with others, and to manifest their abilities in some concrete way in the world. I am passionate about your decision because I believe that a world where people guide their lives consciously and reflectively is a richer, safer, and more creative world. The fact that you are taking your life decisions so seriously says to me that you are head and shoulders above most people, and that your contributions to the world and the people around you will be profound.

To make the *right* decision for yourself, you must bring all of your faculties to bear on the matter. Trust me when I say that the work we will do together will take you far beyond a pros and cons list. Simply by using the analytical tools I provide, you will find a single, logical answer to the question, "Should I go to law school?" You will use your analytic skills to generate data and evaluate alternatives. The thinking part, in fact, is the easy part. You must also use your imagination and your heart to reflect seriously about what law school fulfills for you as a person. I will challenge you and help you to understand your deepest needs and desires – you might also say your deepest purpose – that may or may not be fulfilled in law school or legal practice.

To make the right decision, the decision that you deserve to make at this unique moment in your life, you will need to be profoundly, even shockingly, honest with yourself. My opinion, and I believe the evidence bears me out, is that if you are very unclear about whether or not to go to law school (or to make any major life change, for that matter), it is because you are struggling with your capacity to be honest with yourself and to integrate the information that your honesty surfaces. I realize that this is a blanket statement, and it's not one that I make lightly. But it is an observation and a conviction that comes out of my own lived experience and the experience of many others who have made their way into the legal profession.

Let me give you an example of what I am talking about. I attended law school with the smartest people I have ever met. These are people who graduated with honors from prestigious universities, scored in the 99th percentile on the LSAT, and had a slew of impressive awards and extra-curricular activities. In many conversations with my fellow students, I asked them why they wanted to become lawyers. Numerous people responded with the same comment as one of my classmates: "What else would I do?" His logic was that when he was about to graduate from college he had to figure out what to do with his life to make money. Because there were no obvious alternatives, he decided to go to law school.

Now, I can't speak for his internal processes, but my feeling in the moment was that he was being very honest with me. He faced his choice to go to law school and saw a few things:

- he felt like he had to do something
- he had difficulty devising alternatives
- he didn't feel comfortable simply trying a variety of career options to figure out if one felt better than another

It's entirely possible that he could have taken this thought process much further (and, in fairness, he may have). For example, why did he feel a need to make a life-altering career choice at that particular moment? Did he feel pressure from his parents? Were his peers making these kinds of decisions and he felt pressure to conform? Was he frightened of not knowing what to do and simply wanted to make the feeling of fear go away?

I think all of these are valid reasons to go to law school. I believe, for example, it is okay to go to law school because your parents want you to "do something with your life" and for them that means going to law school or medical school. If you can get to the point where you can be this honest with yourself, you should give yourself a round of applause. It's not easy to translate the drives and impulses that circulate in our brain and our body and make sense of them in such a direct way.

But if this is your reason, it must be done with complete honesty. This means acknowledging to yourself that you are making a major life decision based on someone else's values and timeline. You must also acknowledge that this decision to conform to your parents' wishes may have consequences; for example, long-term resentment of your parents because they didn't encourage you to take the time you needed to figure out a path that made sense for you. Or you may simply be deferring a conversation (i.e. "What matters to me in life?") for another ten years down the road.

Making decisions honestly is important because this is your one life here on Earth. Even if you believe that you will have multiple lives on Earth, that's no excuse not to make the most out of this one. Your life is too precious to casually throw away a decade here and a decade there on decisions that you haven't thought through or that don't deeply make sense to you. If you run with this logic, however, you may start feeling paralyzed. How do you know for sure that *any* decision is the right one?

The good news is that honesty with yourself doesn't require perfection. It's okay to make the wrong decision or to make a decision that makes sense for you now, but in retrospect may seem misguided. It's also okay to take the risk of making a decision just to see where it leads you. My request is that whatever decisions you make, you do so with your eyes wide open. This will steer you away from the most grievous errors and spare you from major regrets.

If you still don't believe that honesty is critically important in your decision to go to law school, that is okay. I think you will still receive immense benefit from the journey of this book and from taking this momentous decision about your future with the curiosity, seriousness and reflection that it deserves.

One thing I know for certain is that law students are among the smartest, energetic and driven people I have met in my life. The fact that you are even considering law school tells me that you are exceptional. My job will be to take the gift of your time, attention, and trust with the seriousness it deserves. When you are finished with this book, your head, heart and gut will all be in alignment. You will have answers that will not just make sense, but that will fundamentally feel right.

HOW TO USE THIS BOOK

The recommended approach to reading this book is to simply read it through from start to finish, completing the exercises as they are presented. If you just can't wait to take advantage of all of the practical information and tools, jump ahead to "Part One: Understanding Your Options." Part One includes all of the information and tools you need to make a rational decision. I call this section "The Simple Answer" because I think that for most people it is easy to get to a point where you have enough data to know whether or not going to law school makes sense (which is only one part of the equation).

But don't stop there. Continue reading "Part Two: Knowing What You Want" to dive deeper into the law school decision. Again, my suggestion to you is that you move through the book linearly to make sure you get the absolute most out of each section.

Throughout this book I will use short-hand terminology to describe various aspects of the law school decision. One of the concepts I will use is the idea of a "top" law school. Many people object to this concept, either because they think ranking systems are flawed or simply because they don't like to see status differentiators between people and their schools. All of that is well and good, but the legal profession takes these status-related considerations seriously. It is simply the truth that it is much easier to get a high-paying legal job when you are at a top-five law school than if you are attending a top twenty-five law school. There are many reasons for this, but one reason is the belief that if you attended a top law school, you also had a great LSAT score and terrific grades. These are predictors of success in law school and, by extension, are predictors of success in your legal career. Given that, you don't have to believe that the rankings themselves are valid to believe that they have real influence in your professional life. So, I will periodically use the term "top law school" with this understanding in mind.

Also in this book, I will periodically make the assumption that you are currently a student with access to your university's career planning resources. I make this assumption because a large percentage of law school applications come from the undergraduate population and because the Junior and Senior years of college are a time when people start thinking seriously about their careers. But this doesn't reflect all law school applicants. Many people have post-graduation work experience before they start considering law school. Others may go to graduate school before applying to law school. If you are currently not a student, I encourage you to contact your alumni association or the career planning office of your *alma mater*. Even though you are no longer affiliated with your school, you may still be allowed access to career planning resources and advice. Regardless of whether you are an undergrad or a full-time worker, this book will greatly aid you in your decision-making process.

To get the most out of this book, read it slowly and in manageable chunks. You will find many sections are densely packed with valuable information and guidance. Take the time to read and reread each chapter until you master the material. Take notes while you read to reinforce the concepts. Be sure to complete the exercises and answer the questions I ask. This book will lead you to an answer that is right for you; but it will only give back to the degree that you put in the right amount of effort.

How much effort is the right amount? Imagine a scale – a giant scale – hanging in the sky. On one end of the scale, put the next ten years of your life: all the people you will meet, the money you will make, the love you will find, the grief and heartache that will befall you, the stress and challenge you will cope with and the milestones you will pass. Imagine your development as a person, the potential you will realize for yourself and the pride you will feel in your accomplishments. But also imagine waking up in the morning wondering how you can face another day of unfulfilled desires, how you can live with the emptiness that continues to burrow its way through your stomach. Imagine all of your possible futures piled sky-high on one end of that giant scale.

On the other end place your efforts today. Each time you look deeply at your life circumstances, the scale starts to balance out. Each moment you look honestly at your desires and capacities, the scale starts to tip in your favor. Every day, every week and every month you own your life and take complete responsibility for your decisions, you set in motion a momentum that propels your life in a positive direction. Only you can know how much effort is the right amount of effort. One thing I'm certain of is that your life is utterly worth your dedicated, tenacious and patient attention.

Because there are many gatekeepers that control access to the legal profession, it's easy to forget that the legal profession needs to measure up to *your* criteria, not the other way around.

PART ONE

UNDERSTANDING YOUR OPTIONS

This section presents the Simple Answer to the question of whether or not you should go to law school. By Simple Answer, I mean an answer that is purely driven by data and reasonable extrapolation. We're going to break down the information at your disposal piece-by-piece and come up with a custom-tailored law school decision just for you. We'll look at the facts that are publicly available – such as law school tuition and starting salaries after law school – as well as the facts that are unique to you. If the law school decision is purely an analytic decision for you, this chapter will provide 100% of the information you need to come up with an answer.

The thesis behind this book is that for those of you who are genuinely unsure about your law school decision, it's not just about the Simple Answer. Your motivations are complex and require more nuanced consideration than an Excel spreadsheet will yield. But even if your decision is not entirely about the Simple Answer, it doesn't mean that a purely analytic consideration of your decision is irrelevant. It's actually extremely important and can reveal new information for you about needs and interests you have not yet articulated.

CHAPTER ONE

RETURN ON INVESTMENT (ROI)

Return on Investment (ROI) is a business term that is useful in comparing business opportunities. If you have two competing investment opportunities, you can compare the ROI for each investment (as measured in net present value) to determine the best way to spend your money. The ROI for an investment, in simple terms, is the present value of the cash the investment will generate, less the initial investment itself. If you invest $500 in purchasing a stock that doubles in value over 5 years, your ROI will be the present value of the $1,000 sale price five years from now less your original investment of $500. (I mention "present value" because money changes in value over time. In general, a dollar today is worth more than a dollar five years from now due to various factors, for example, inflation.) ROI is generally expressed as a percentage – i.e. an investment may have a 10% ROI.

We can use this idea in thinking about the law school decision. If working with numbers is not your *forte*, don't worry – we'll take everything step–by–step and you may not need to go too deeply to come up with an answer.

When thinking about the ROI of law school, imagine a machine with many levers. As you move each lever up or down, you affect your overall ROI. When consdering attending law school, the key levers are as follows:

TUITION COST You can measure this in the total actual cost of tuition to you. If you are paying out–of–pocket, this will mean the cash you are parting with to attend law school. If you are taking on student loans, this would include the total cost of the loan over the life of the loan (generally 1.25 to 2.25 times the amount of money you borrow, depending on the length of the loan and your interest rate). If you receive a scholarship, you should subtract your scholarship amount from your tuition cost.

LIVING EXPENSES You still have to eat and pay rent while you are in law school (unless you already own your own home). Whether you live like royalty or like a peasant is up to you. When calculating living expenses, stick with the big ticket items like rent and then add an average monthly amount for all other expenses. In many universities, health insurance will be covered as part of your student fees. If this is not the case for your law school, add an additional amount to your monthly budget for health insurance.

OPPORTUNITY COST Opportunity Cost is your lost income during law school. If you could earn $150,000 working for three years instead of attending law school, that is your lost income. Opportunity cost can also include the income that you would have earned *after* three years if you had not attended law school.

AVERAGE STARTING SALARY You can find this out on any number of web sites or from the schools you are applying to. Each school will have different starting salaries based on its reputation and geographic location. This amount will vary dramatically if you are working for a law firm vs. practicing public interest law (i.e. working for a non-profit or NGO) vs. government work.[1]

YEARS IN LEGAL PRACTICE This is the number of years you intend to practice law after you leave law school. This may be difficult to know in advance. If you are not sure, use the general average of about five years.

1 There is significant controversy over the reliability of data regarding starting salaries and placement rates. There is much discussion on the web about whether law schools report this information accurately or whether the data is skewed by the number of students who actually complete salary surveys. For example, if only the students who receive job offers report their earnings, it may seem like a particular law school has higher placement rates and starting salaries than is actually the case.

Each of these attributes changes ROI. For example, as *tuition cost* increases, ROI decreases (unless *average starting salary* also increases). Higher *tuition cost* means you are investing more without necessarily increasing your revenue. As *years in legal practice* increases, ROI may increase assuming an alternative career would not provide an equal or greater income. This is because you have more time to recoup your original investment. There are certainly more levers to this ROI machine (such as cost of textbooks, revenue from summer internships, length of time to pay off student loans, etc.), but getting a handle on these big numbers is sufficient for most people.

You can go as deep as you like with ROI analysis, but sometimes the equation is quite simple. For example, if you are pursuing a public interest career where your starting salary is $60,000, investing in a $100,000 legal education is a bad idea financially. You will likely never recoup your original investment because you could make just as much money pursuing a non-legal career path (and not going $100,000 into debt in the first place). Of course, you may not be going to law school for financial reasons in this case; but it demonstrates that for some career paths almost no math is required to realize a legal career has less ROI than other career paths.

On the other extreme, if you get a full scholarship to Harvard, Stanford, or Yale; are interested in living in San Francisco or Manhattan; and currently have no marketable skills, your ROI looks pretty good. Think about this piece-by-piece: if your tuition cost is zero, your starting salary is $120,000 and your opportunity cost is $60,000 (assuming you could have earned $20,000 per year for three years if you had not attended law school), you will have positive ROI even if you just practice law for a year. In simple terms, you are investing $80,000 in opportunity cost (i.e. $20,000 per year for the three years you are in law school and another $20,000 for the first year out of law school) to make $120,000. This is not a bad investment.

Let's take a more middle-of-the road example. I'm going to walk through the numbers for a hypothetical student attending a top law school. This process is the same process that you should go through for yourself. So, read through this example to get the idea and then walk through it again using the numbers that are appropriate for you.

SAMPLE ANALYSIS

Wendy is graduating from Stanford University with an undergraduate degree in Economics. Wendy has applied to a number of law schools and has been lucky enough to get into a top school, in her case, Stanford Law School. This is great for Wendy because she has a strong desire to remain in the San Francisco Bay Area.

The first thing Wendy does to evaluate her decision is gather some important data. First off is tuition cost. The tuition for Stanford Law School in the 2009-2010 school year was $42,420. Let's take that as a starting point. If you choose to live on campus, you will spend another $18,603. (Living off campus will likely be more expensive, though it may also be more desirable.) Your books will cost an additional $1,815. The Stanford Law School web site estimates that a single student (i.e. no dependents) will need to budget $67,359 for the school year. They have estimated a little over $1,200 for clothing, transportation, and recreation. The website also estimates $3,300 for a new laptop computer (which is required). Of course, if you own a car, $1,200 is barely enough to cover gas for a year, so I would go with a higher number just to play it safe. Let's assume that Wendy thinks $70,000 is a reasonable number that she can live with.

Fortunately, Stanford provides need-based scholarships to 80 percent of its students, averaging $20,000 per student.[1] So, Wendy's annual investment will be closer to $50,000. Over three years, that totals to a $150,000 investment. Wendy doesn't have any personal savings, so she will have to borrow this money. If she takes ten years to pay off the loan at a 6.8% rate (the current rate for a Stafford loan), she will pay approximately $40,000 in interest and fees over the life of the loan. If she were to take 30 years to pay off the loan, she would pay $134,000 in interest and fees over the life of the loan. Wendy is ambitious and thinks she will pay off the loan in ten years. So, her net investment will be $150,000 in tuition plus $40,000 in interest, or $190,000.

What is Wendy giving up by going to law school? Her opportunity cost is her lost income while she is in law school. It is very difficult, if not impossible, to work while in law school, and Wendy is choosing to focus on her studies rather than trying to hold down a job. Because she is very enterprising and wants to work in the San Francisco area, Wendy knows that she could make at least $60,000 after she graduates from college if she does not pursue a law degree.[2] Assuming she will receive a 10% pay increase per year (again, she is hard-working and bright), she will make $66,000 in year two and $72,600 in year three. The opportunity cost in going to law school for Wendy, then, is $198,000. Added to her tuition cost, Wendy will graduate from law school $388,000 behind.

1 This information will change from year to year. See your individual law school's site for more accurate information. The data I am using for Stanford Law School comes from their web site at http://www.law.stanford.edu/program/tuition/.

2 In the 2007-2008 graduating class, students from Stanford University with Bachelor's degrees had average starting salaries of $59,379. Your school's career placement office should have data that is relevant for recent graduating classes from your university. If this information is unavailable, use the Internet to find starting salaries in your region.

The next step is to figure out average starting salaries. Wendy is interested in a corporate law job and hopes to work at a large law firm in San Francisco. The latest stats on the Stanford Law School web site say that the average starting salary for those working at law firms in 2007 was $160,000. Of course, 2007 was a long time ago. Based on economic conditions, starting salaries may have changed. For now, this is the latest information that Wendy has, so let's stick with it. Of course, Wendy's salary won't be stuck at $160,000 forever. The longer she is with her firm, her salary will increase. By year five, she may make over $200,000 in annual income.[3]

She can't do anything with the starting salary information until she figures out the last factor: How many years does she plan to practice law? Wendy's sense of things is that she'll practice law for the rest of her working life. But it's hard to know this for sure, given that she hasn't even started law school yet.

The question of attrition at law firms continues to be studied. Currently, it is fair to say that there is a very high level of attrition at large law firms when associates are five years out from law school. So, Wendy decides to assume for the purpose of this analysis that she will have a high-paying law firm job for five years after she graduates.[4]

Now Wendy has all the numbers she needs to understand whether law school is a good investment. She makes a table that tracks her earnings over her first five years out of law school. She needs to compare this with her earnings if she does not attend law school. For the sake of ease, Wendy assumes she will have a 10% pay increase each year regardless of her career path. Here is what she comes up with:

	1	2	3	4	5	Total
Legal Job	$160,000	$176,000	$193,600	$212,960	$234,256	$976,816
Non-Legal Job	$79,860	$87,846	$96,630	$106,293	$116,923	$487,552

What this analysis tells Wendy is that in her law firm job, she will earn $489,264 more than if she had not pursued a legal career. This sounds great, but Wendy also needs to subtract the $388,000 that reflects the costs of her school debt and opportunity cost. She finds that if all goes as planned, she will still come out $101,263 ahead after five years by pursuing a law degree. This is slightly less than the amount of money she would have made by simply investing $388,000 over five years and earning 5% on her investment each year. Her situation seems worse by considering

3 This information is based on current data on San Francisco Bay Area salaries at large law firms. Wendy's experience may be different from yours if you don't plan on attending a top law school or working in a major legal market.

4 For more on this topic, see my blog post "How Long Does Your Law School Decision Last?" at http://thelawschooldecision.com/2010/02/06/how-long-does-your-law-school-decision-last/.

tax implications. All of these salary numbers are gross income (i.e. her salary before taxes are taken out). In general, the more money you earn in salary, the more income tax you pay. So, her actual net return over her three years of law school and five years of working as an attorney will certainly be far less than $101,263.

So, is this a good investment for Wendy? On its face, the answer is "no." Wendy works very hard for eight years, making many personal sacrifices, all to make less than a 5% return on her investment. But, it is worthwhile to do this exercise several times, changing the assumptions. For example, what if Wendy's starting salary is 20% lower, but she works in legal practice for an additional three years? What if Wendy were to attend a cheaper school than Stanford? What would her starting salary be then and how would this affect her ROI? What if Wendy decides to move to another city where starting salaries within and outside of law are much lower?

Wendy can also consider the question from a slightly different angle: If she is passionate about practicing law, is the personal fulfillment she gets out of her career worth making an investment with a modest return? Those less quantifiable aspects will be explored more in Chapter Two. However, they are worth mentioning as a valid consideration when assessing ROI in the context of career choices.

Of course, this analysis is extremely hypothetical. Anything could happen in Wendy's life. If she doesn't go to law school, she could work for a start-up company that becomes terrifically successful; if she does go to law school, she could make legal practice a life-long career; she could be in a car accident that prevents her from being able to go to law school or work at all.

It's hard to say exactly how things would play out for Wendy. However, just because life is unpredictable, it doesn't mean that you are off the hook for thinking about this life decision very carefully. Running the numbers helps you think about this choice from an extremely practical perspective. It orients you to the idea that however you spend your time, you are making trade-offs. It helps you think about what school to attend, what kind of job you want, and the total cost of law school debt. Understanding those trade-offs and their potential consequences will make you an extremely lucid decision-maker when it comes to practical matters.

CHAPTER TWO

IDENTIFYING ATTRIBUTES AND DEFINING SUCCESS CRITERIA

You now know how to tell if law school is a good investment. Now, let's turn our attention to legal practice and ask the question: Will practicing law meet your career and lifestyle objectives? Answering this question involves four steps:

1. Identify attributes
2. Define success criteria
3. Gather data
4. Evaluate data

We'll walk through each of these steps together and I'll provide you with some sample answers that reflect a typical profile of a law school applicant.

THE EVALUATION PROCESS

What is important to you in a career? To analyze whether or not the legal profession is a fit for you, you need to develop a sense of what matters to you career-wise. If you don't know what is important to you, there is no way of measuring whether or not legal practice will fulfill your desires.

Because there are many gatekeepers that control access to the legal profession (the LSAT, your law school admissions office, your state bar, etc.), it's easy to forget that the legal profession needs to measure up to *your* criteria, not the other way around. The legal profession should prove its worth to *you* before you start trying to prove your worth to it.

If you haven't thought much about what you want from a career, it's time to do some brainstorming. For most law school applicants, the following questions are already on their minds:

- How much money will I make?
- How many hours will I have to work?
- What is the nature of the work I will be doing as a lawyer?
- How stable is this career path?

As career attributes, we can distill these down to: money, hours per week, activities, and stability. Whether or not you think this is a comprehensive list, you should take some time – preferably right now – to come up with your own list. I can imagine a number of questions that might not apply to everyone, but may be relevant for you. For example, do any of the following apply to you?

- I want to start a family. Is legal practice flexible enough to accommodate my parenting interests?
- I want to work as a politician or as a political advisor. Will a law degree help me succeed in this area?
- Will law school or legal practice require that I relocate?
- What are the opportunities for promotion and job growth in law?
- Is practicing law fun/interesting/fulfilling?
- Can I work for myself? Or do I need to work for a firm?
- What legal career paths involve appearing in court vs. working behind a desk?
- My background/personality/lifestyle is different from the norm. Will I have an equal chance at success and promotion in the legal profession?
- Can I make a difference in the world on this career path?

These questions are provided to stimulate your thinking, but you should really spend time understanding your own needs. For some people, the important attributes will be extremely simple, for example, money and stability. For others, it will be fruitful to really dig in to what is important to you in a career. Imagine that the legal profession is auditioning for a role in your play (i.e. your life). What questions would you ask of the legal profession before you cast it in the role of your career path?

Identifying attributes is simply the process of identifying what is important to you in a career path. When you develop your list of attributes, think about what you want from a career path in general rather than from law in particular. If you believe that any profession you choose should allow you to show up to work in clown makeup, add that to your list even if you don't think it is realistic in legal practice. Our goal here is to find out whether or not law measures up to your own standards for career value. Nothing should be considered off the table in this analysis as long as it is important to you.

Once you have identified the attributes that are important to you, it's time to determine success criteria. A success criterion is just a measure of what represents a passing grade for each attribute. For example, for money, your success criterion may be: "I want have an annual income of at least $120,000 five years from now." You might also consider a low/medium/high grade for each attribute. For example, "I would love to earn more than $150,000, I would accept earning $100,000 and I could live with earning $80,000 for a short time." Success criteria tell you if the requirement for each attribute has been met. Some success criteria may be binary (i.e. a "yes" or "no" answer). An example criterion would be, "I want to work no more than 40 hours a week so that I can start a family and enjoy parenting." If you simply won't be happy otherwise, you can exclude career paths that require more than 40 hours of work per week.

Once you have established your success criteria, it's time to gather data. There are three essential resources for you in this endeavor:

- The Internet
- Your college career office
- Informational interviews

The Internet can be a useful source of information for statistical data such as average starting salaries for graduating classes at particular law schools or salaries over five years at particular law firms. As you do your research on the Internet, it's a good idea to be geographically specific and law school specific. These are two factors that have a dramatic impact on placement and salary levels in the legal profession. If you read, for example, that lawyers have an average starting salary of $60,000, you should immediately ask "In what markets?" and "With a degree from which school?" As always, make sure your data is coming from reasonably credible sources.

The college career office is an often overlooked treasure trove of useful information about career options. Depending on how well resourced your career office is, it may be able to provide you with better information than you can find on the Internet alone. Your career office may subscribe to industry journals or reports that you are unlikely to purchase for yourself. Career counselors can help you think of strategies for finding the data you need. (Your librarian may help you with this as well.) Most important, your career office will be able to connect you with alumni who are currently practicing law and may be willing to speak with you about the legal career path.

This latter point is referred to as "informational interviewing", which I also discuss in Part Two and the Addendum. For now, think of informational interviewing as a chance to gather data from people who are currently working in law. Informational interviews can happen over the phone or in person and should be driven by your list of attributes.

Imagine that your interviewee is actually representing the legal profession. Ask them about the points that are most important to you in a career and listen to their answers carefully. Don't be shy about asking questions or explaining your agenda (i.e. "I'm considering going to law school and I want to ask a practicing lawyer some questions about the legal career path.").

A few notes about the etiquette of gathering data in this way. If you are interested in asking about money, I suggest that you don't directly ask your interviewee how much they make. Instead, you can ask, "How much do starting associates make in your firm?" or "Do attorneys typically have bonus structures built in to their compensation packages?"

Enjoy these interviews and always express appreciation for your interviewee's time. In addition to thanking them verbally, send a thank-you note. An email thank-you note is probably enough. But a written thank-you note is a great sign of appreciation. In any case, expressing your appreciation is a non-optional part of this process.[5]

Finally, while informational interviews are essential, don't put undue weight on the data you gather. If an interviewee tells you "Becoming a lawyer is the worst mis-

5 Be sure to review the "Tips on Informational Interviewing" addendum to this guide.

take you could possibly make" or "You should definitely become a lawyer if you are smart and want to make a lot of money," take it simply as information about the individual you are interviewing. It's fair to assume that the person you talk to isn't the only one who has that particular opinion. But it's good to blend your interview data with data from other sources (such as statistics from your potential law school career office).

Why conduct informational interviews if you shouldn't generalize about the data you gather? The goal of the informational interview isn't necessarily to gather statistical evidence; rather, it is an opportunity for you to discuss and explore your priorities with someone who is already in the business of law. The interactive context of the interview may help you clarify your values or give you the data you need to refine your success criteria.

Once you have gathered the data you need, it's time to evaluate. Evaluation could be as simple as a checklist that produces an obvious answer. For some people this will be the case. For example, if you want to make $100,000 a year in five years and you don't want to relocate, you shouldn't be an attorney if you live outside of a major legal market (such as San Francisco or New York). Instead, you should identify more lucrative career paths in your local area.

For other people, the outcome won't be entirely obvious. For example, imagine that you want to make $120,000 in annual income five years from now. You live in a legal market where this is theoretically possible. But you aren't sure that you have the LSAT score or the grades that will get you into a law school from which the big firms hire. This might be an opportunity to surface additional attributes or success criteria. For example, "Success should be possible in this career path for people who don't score well on tests."

In the evaluation step, you are determining whether or not the legal profession meets your requirements for a career path that could be acceptable for you. If you find that the legal profession meets your requirements, this still doesn't mean that you should go to law school. What it means is that law school is at the least in the running for consideration as a potential career choice. Later, we will try to determine what differentiates law from other career paths that could also meet all of your requirements.

COMMON CAREER ATTRIBUTES

Let's consider each of the common career attributes listed above. For each of them, we will develop success criteria and compare them to the actual data we find from the Internet and informational interviews.

MONEY

How much money do you want to make? Unless you are independently wealthy, you will need to make money of some kind to pay for housing, clothing, and food. You may also want more than that – a nice car, the ability to travel and take vacations, and the ability to buy your own home. You may even be dreaming bigger. Do you want to own multiple homes? Do you want to create your own foundation? Do you want to be able to afford to take several months off from working each year? Do you want to have kids? If so, will they go to public school or private school? How much will you need to save for their college educations?

It may be hard at this moment in your life to know exactly how much money you want to make. People tend to be anchored in their current income range. For example, if you currently make $20,000 per year, it may seem like $50,000 will give you all that you possibly need to live comfortably. If you make $50,000 per year, $75,000 might sound luxurious. It's much harder to make bigger imaginative leaps. For example, if you make $20,000 per year, why not imagine making $2,000,000 or $20,000,000?

There are at least two reasons why this is hard to imagine: First, you are currently thinking about life in terms of day-to-day decisions that are calibrated to your current income level. If you struggle to pay rent, it's hard to imagine what it's like to easily afford mortgages on your main residence and your vacation homes in Maui and Paris. If your current tuition bill makes your jaw drop, it's hard to think about having a personal chef and your own housekeeper. Second, because you may not know *how* to get from $20,000 to $20,000,000, it may seem like an unrealistic fantasy to even consider the possibility. Given this, when you are imagining how much money you want to make (assuming money is important to you), you should stretch your imagination, but not so much that your aspiration seems completely unbelievable. As you approach your ideal income, it will become easier to reach further and create more ambitious goals for yourself.

One more note about money: Are you comfortable *thinking* about your financial goals and desires? For some, the objective of making money may seem superficial, status-driven, or greedy. As such, the idea of buying a helicopter may seem excessive and ostentatious. Some who pursue public interest careers helping the less financially fortunate in our society may see the accumulation of wealth as something that comes at the expense of others. If money is a source of harm, it might make sense to avoid wanting too much of it.

The desire for money, however, is not inherently harmful to oneself or others. It is true that the pursuit of money – when it comes at the expense of all other things – can limit the complete expression of your personality. It can cause you to make personal and ethical decisions that you might not otherwise make if money weren't your primary motivation. But complicated, self-destructive motivations are not limited to those who seek money. In all walks of life, people limit their potential, subdue their compassion, and act cruelly toward each other. While these behaviors sometimes go hand-in-hand with the pursuit of money, the desire for money is not the underlying cause.

The pursuit of money can in fact have salubrious influence on individuals and society. Many pursue money as an expression of their aptitudes and resourcefulness. They relish their ability to take care of themselves financially, to explore the world, and to express their generosity through philanthropy or service. Seeking wealth is an act of self-care that enriches their personalities and builds their resilience. Wanting more things – like a vacation home in Maui – can be an expression of imagination and creativity. It can be a source of inspiration during difficult times and can help you take on difficult tasks knowing that you will be rewarded in the future. Suppressing the desire for wealth may simply serve to suppress the parts of your personality that are hungry for vitality, hungry for ease or hungry for care. Denying your desires for money (or the things that money buys) distorts your personality rather than giving you room to explore and understand your needs and wishes.

Whether or not you find it easy to agree with what I've said, it is nonetheless certain that money will be part of most people's evaluation of law school. To get concrete about how much money you want, start by imagining an annual income meets the following criteria:

- Your income addresses your practical needs.
- Your income supports the lifestyle that you want.
- Your income is at least a little bit more than currently seems possible.

To ensure that your number meets your practical needs, you could determine how much rent, clothing, and food costs in the area where you want to live. You could develop a monthly budget based on your desired income. But instead of doing that, let's take a short cut: Find out what the average household income is in your area.

For example, according to U.S. Census data, the median household income in the San Francisco Bay Area in 2007 was $67,333. We can assume that this is how much it takes to support one or two people in this geographical area. You can consider the median household income as your baseline (unless, for some reason, you aspire to earn less than average).

The second point is that your income should support the lifestyle you want. Your lifestyle is up to you. Do you like to buy new clothes and go out to eat at restaurants? Or do you love going to second-hand clothing stores and making most of your meals at home? These are different lifestyles and each costs a different amount of money. If you are in the first group, figure out how much spending money you need each month and multiply it by the number of months in a year. If you are in the latter group, you can probably stick with the median income in your area. Some may also consider the idea of savings and investment. Add to your monthly budget the amount that you would like to put into savings or investment opportunities.

To work with something concrete, let's imagine that you want a budget of $1,000 each month to buy things and you want to save or invest $1,500 per month. You might be able to avoid being taxed on your savings (if you invest in a retirement account), but your spending money will need to be post-tax dollars. This means that you would need to earn around $16,800 in order to have $10,000 left per year for spending money. Over twelve months, this would add $34,800 to your annual income requirement, i.e. $18,000 for savings and $16,800 for fun. In the San Francisco area, this would mean that you would need to earn around $102,000 per year.

To the final point, you should determine whether the number you arrived at in step two is a stretch for you. Realize that, as you make more money, your norms about what "a lot" of money means will change. If $102,000 already seems like a lot of money, you're set. But test it with a higher number – does making $125,000 seem at all possible to imagine? If so, go with the higher number. The idea here is that you want to create a number in steps one and two and then make sure you aren't shortchanging yourself in step three. Your future is fairly unknown at this point in time; but I assure you that if you put your mind to it, you can make any amount of money you want. Now is the time to start stretching your ability to imagine how much money is possible for you.

Let's imagine that $125,000 sounds like an imaginable amount of money, but still a pretty big stretch. If that is the case, the success criterion for the "money" attribute is $125,000. That means that for the legal profession to meet your requirements, it must provide you with a job that minimally allows you to earn $125,000 per year.

Take some time to figure out what *your* success criterion for money is. When you have a number, say it out loud: "Legal Profession, prove to me that you can provide me with at least X amount of dollars each year," where X is your success criterion for money.

Once you have done this, it's time to gather data about the legal profession. For money, this is pretty easy. The law schools that you are applying to should provide you with placement statistics (i.e. what percent of the graduating class graduates with job offers) and salary information. You can find this on the web site for each law school or in the application packet that the law school sends to you. Keep in mind that this data can vary dramatically from school to school. Top schools may have a 95% placement rate and starting salaries well over $100,000 per year. Other schools may have 50% placement rates with starting salaries around $60,000. This variation could reflect the overall status of the school or the geographic area where most students get placed upon graduation.[6]

Note that you should take risk into account when quantifying the "average starting salary." For example, if 50% of the graduates from your school get placed in jobs making $65,000 per year, you should treat the average starting salary as $32,500. It may be tempting to assume that you will most certainly be among the 50% of graduates who get job offers; but, from a purely quantitative perspective, it's not honest.

Once you have gathered the necessary data, it is easy to evaluate. If you need to make $100,000 per year, but graduates from your chosen or desired law school only have average starting salaries of $75,000, law might not be the right career path for you. If, on the other hand, graduates from your school of choice make well over $100,000 on average, the legal profession is looking good. Of course, the money question may not be the sole or even the most important attribute for you when considering a career in law. But for some people, it is.

If your earning potential is an important consideration for you, it is essential that you know how much money you want and determine if the legal profession can give it to you. (It is also important to read the ROI section of this guide, as a full evaluation of the financial rewards of law school is incomplete without it.) In any case, money can be a useful disqualifying factor if the law school you want to go to doesn't produce graduates who make as much money as you want to make.

HOURS PER WEEK

How *much* do you want to work? Some people love working non-stop. In a way, work calms them and they are otherwise anxious or undirected if their free time

6 Refer back to my note above on the controversy over the accuracy of this data.

isn't structured by work activities. Other people may appreciate some aspects of work, but also place high value on their leisure time. For this group, family, friends, hobbies or other forms of expression are essential parts of their lives. And, of course, a good many people would rather not go to work at all.

Developing success criteria for hours per week is a little tricky. It may be true that you want to make at least $200,000 per year, but you don't want to work more than an hour per day. This is extremely useful information about your preferences. It's clear that you want to live richly, but are also averse to working. The problem, though, is that working five hours per week is not a great success criterion for those who are not independently wealthy. There are very few job opportunities – and I would venture to say almost none in the legal profession – that afford this amount of time off while still paying a high wage. So, what to do?

The approach here is to think about this requirement in conjunction with the money requirement. Work backward from the money you want to make to determine the amount of time you are willing to invest. As an extreme example, would you be willing to work 100 hours per week for a year if you could make $5,000,000? Many would be willing to take on this short-term sacrifice in order to gain a great financial reward. In the case of your requirement for the legal profession, let's imagine that you need to get paid $125,000 per year after you graduate from law school. How hard would you be willing to work in order to make that much money?

To help you determine the number of hours that is right for you, let's walk through a few scenarios. These scenarios will assume that you need eight hours of sleep per day (may not be true for everyone) and that you spend one-half hour at work eating lunch, making coffee, using the restroom, and other non-work activities. The standard work week in the United States is a 40-hour work week. In the 40-hour work week, your day may look like this:

What Time Is It?	Activity	Allocated Time
7:00 am	Wake-Up, Eat Breakfast, Shower	1 hour
8:00 am	Drive to work	30 minutes
8:30 am	Work	8.5 hour
5:00 pm	Drive home; go to the grocery store	1 hour
6:00 pm	Eat dinner; spend time with family and friends; pursue hobbies; watch movies and TV; answer personal email; clean house	5 hours
11:00 pm	Go to bed	8 hours

You repeat this schedule five days per week and you spend most weekends in self-guided activities. Note that in the 40-hour week, work takes up most of your day. Sleep is in a close second and relaxing is a solid third.

What does a 50-hour work week look like? If you only work five days a week, it looks like this:

What Time Is It?	Activity	Allocated Time
7:00 am	Wake-Up, Eat Breakfast, Shower	1 hour
8:00 am	Drive to work	30 minutes
8:30 am	Work	10.5 hours
7:00 pm	Drive home; go to the grocery store	1 hour
8:00 pm	Eat dinner; spend time with family and friends; pursue hobbies; watch movies and TV; answer personal email; clean house	3 hours
11:00 pm	Go to bed	8 hours

In this scenario, you end up with about three hours per day in leisure activities. This is enough time to eat dinner, talk on the phone to a friend and watch a TV show. You could also just work 9.5 hours per day and work an extra five hours on the weekend.

Let's continue with a 60-hour work week:

What Time Is It?	Activity	Allocated Time
7:00 am	Wake-Up, Eat Breakfast, Shower	1 hour
8:00 am	Drive to work	30 minutes
8:30 am	Work	10.5 hours
7:00 pm	Drive home; go to the grocery store	1 hour
8:00 pm	Eat dinner; spend time with family and friends; pursue hobbies; watch movies and TV; answer personal email; clean house	3 hours
11:00 pm	Go to bed	8 hours

This looks exactly the same as the 50-hour week, only you are following this schedule six days per week. That gives you Sunday to sleep, relax, and get ready to go again on Monday. If you really wanted more time on the weekend, you could work eleven and a half hours, five days a week (55 hours) and then work five hours on Saturday. This would give you two hours each weekday evening to eat, straighten up the house, and watch a sit-com on TV.

For the 70-hour work week, imagine working 10.5 hours per day, seven days a week. That means you have about 3 hours per day to spend with yourself and you have no additional time on the weekends. You could also work twelve hours a day, five days a week and then work a ten-hour day on Saturday. Some jobs may require that you work more, but let's imagine that a 70-hour work week over a prolonged period of time is at the limits of what is sustainable for anyone.

What does your day look like today? If you have a full-time job currently, it will be easy to compare these various schedules to your own. If you are a student, figure out the total time you spend in class and seriously studying each day. How many hours per week do you currently work?

To decide how much you want to work, first spend some time seriously imagining the schedules above. How important is it for you to spend time socializing? Are there other activities outside of work that may be important to you? Or is work typically the most compelling thing in your life and you have a strong passion for work activities? Spend a few moments imagining each schedule in detail. How will it feel to wake up in the morning in each scenario? What thoughts will be going through your head as you get ready to go to work? When you get home at night, how will you feel? What will you look forward to each day? What will you tell your friends about your day in each scenario?

Now imagine what you would be willing to give up financially in order to reclaim some of your personal time. For example, if you could make $125,000 working 70 hours a week or $100,000 working 40 hours a week, which would you choose? Would you give up $25,000 (in pre-tax dollars) in order to get back 30 hours per week? Over the course of the year, that is 1,560 hours or $16 per hour. Would you be willing to pay $16 per hour in order to reclaim 1,560 hours for yourself each year? Play with these scenarios until you have a feel for how much you would be willing to work each week and still lead the life that you want. Again, the question you are asking yourself is – given the trade-offs, how many hours per week am I willing to work in order to make the amount of money I want to make? Your answer will be your success criterion, expressed in hours per week.

Hours per week is a particularly relevant measure in the legal profession. Law firms make money and, hence, pay salaries, rent, and partner profits by billing their clients. Firms bill clients at an hourly rate for work performed. A legal associate may, for example, bill out at $150 per hour. This doesn't mean that the associate gets paid this much. Rather, the $150 per hour reflects many of the firm's costs, including:

- Your salary
- Salaries for support staff (legal secretaries, IT staff, mail clerks,

accountants, etc.)

- Rent (often in high-rent, downtown areas)
- Equipment (computers, copy machines, etc.)
- Recruiting new attorneys
- Marketing to potential clients
- Entertaining existing and potential clients
- Research libraries
- Malpractice insurance
- Performing pro-bono work
- Profits

In fact, law firms have so many expenses, the $150 per hour rate may seem far too little to pay for their actual costs. How do firms deal with this? They require (implicitly or explicitly) that lawyers bill a minimum number of hours each year. This minimum number averages between 1,700 and 2,300 hours per year. The minimum number of hours you are required to bill is a function of the legal market you are in (for example, New York vs. Kansas City), the size of the firm you work for and how much money you make. A billable hour means an hour working directly on a client matter – it doesn't include coffee breaks, lunch or dinner, bathroom breaks, checking email (unless the emails are directly related to the client), attending company meetings, attending trainings, staying up-to-date on new legislation or court cases, taking clients or prospects out to dinner or your daily commute to and from work.

The Yale Law School Career Development Office has published an analysis of the billable hour on their web site that provides sample estimates of billable hour requirements vs. actual hours worked. On the low end, they estimate that to bill 1,800 hours, you must actually work 51 hours per week, not including your commute. To bill 2,200 hours, they estimate that you will work between 65 and 70 hours per week. These estimates assume that you never experience a prolonged illness or have other personal matters that will diminish your productivity. It also assumes that you aspire to mediocrity. Remember that these are minimums we are talking about. If you aspire to make partner, you might be motivated to work extra hard to generate even more profit for the firm.[7]

Whether or how billable hours factor into your career path depends on how much money you want to make and the environment you work in. For example, if you

7 For the Yale Law School Career Development Office analysis, see "The Truth About the Billable Hour" here: http://www.law.yale.edu/documents/pdf/CDO_Public/cdo-billable_hour.pdf. This analysis is so interesting, I have archived a copy in my reference library. If the document is no longer available on the web site as you are reading this, feel free to contact my support email address and I will have the document emailed to you.

work in a legal role for the government or a public interest organization, you may escape billable hours as a concern (and you will also make significantly less money). If you work in a large law firm in a major metropolitan area, billing hours will always be on your mind. Medium-size firms may have billable hours on the lower end of the scale. These "lifestyle" firms will also pay less money and may not provide paths to partnership. In a sense, billable hours is an extremely rational measure: The harder you work, the more profit you will generate for your firm and the more money you will ultimately make.

With this in mind, it's a good idea to talk to practicing attorneys that are working in environments that you can see yourself in. If you imagine practicing law in a big firm, talk to someone who already is working in a firm. If you imagine working in an environmental advocacy role at an NGO, talk to someone who is already in that role. Unlike asking about someone's salary, it is perfectly acceptable to ask someone about their live/work balance. Ask how many hours they work each week, what time they have for personal interests and relationships, how long they have been working at their current level and how long they think they can sustain their current work level. In the process of talking to people, you will get a feel for what an attorney's life is like and how it fits with your own vision for your life.

Once you have gathered data, it's time to evaluate. Will the legal career path of your choice allow you to work your desired number of hours per week and pay you the amount of money you would like to get paid? I encourage you to treat this point as dead serious. So many attorneys don't truly visualize what it is like to work a 60- or 70-hour work week until they have invested three years in their legal education and have a mountain of debt to pay off.

Now is the time to really think seriously about the kind of life you want for yourself. If you think you will be passionate about practicing law and it will deeply feed you, nourish you, and express your capacities brilliantly, it might make sense to work 60 hours a week immersed in your passion. But if you are considering law school because you are not sure what else to do with your life, it is essential that you think clearly about how you will feel when the alarm goes off at six o'clock in the morning and you are getting ready for another ten- to twelve-hour work day. Make it real for yourself such that you are thinking the thoughts and feeling the feelings of a very hard–working attorney.

One final note about hours per week: Don't let the norms of the legal profession influence your thinking about the number of hours per week you are willing to work. Remember our original orientation: Your task is to decide the maximum number of hours per week you are willing to work in order to make a specific amount of money. The legal profession can either meet your criterion or not; but, you should evaluate opportunities in law on your own terms rather than using legal norms to shape your sense of what is acceptable.

ACTIVITIES

What do you want to do each day at work? If you are considering law school, it's likely that you are interested in work that has the feel of school. Reading, studying, mastering new material, and writing might be the ideal activities for you. But be sure to consider other facets of your personality that might be interesting to you. How important is social interaction for you? Can you work in relative solitude all day? Or do you prefer to brainstorm or talk through problems with other people? How creative do you like your work to feel? How much physical movement do you like to have each day? Would you feel more fulfilled opening a martial arts studio, developing new iPhone applications or writing up legal agreements?

To start answering these questions, think about the things that you currently enjoy. Do you play sports? Do you like to dance? In other jobs you've had or in student organizations you've belonged to, what role do you play? Is it fun for you to interact with customers and co-workers? How much do you enjoy solitary activities, like sitting at home and reading a book? What is your need for variation in your day? Do you like to do many small activities or would you prefer to do one extended activity?

There are countless questions that you could ask yourself to better understand your preferred work style. I highly suggest you take a personality inventory like Myers-Briggs to better understand your personality and how that may translate into fitting professions. (It's likely that your campus career center can provide you with free or low-cost opportunities to take one of these highly-respected assessments.) To simplify the problem in the interest of developing success criteria, let's consider the following dimensions of work activities:

- Group vs. Solitary
- Sedentary vs. Active
- Analytic vs. Creative
- Focused vs. Varied

GROUP VS. SOLITARY

Some people prefer group activities to solitary activities. Group activities are any activities that involve interaction with at least one other individual, in person or over the phone. Group activities include brainstorming, troubleshooting, customer service, sales, presentations and planning. (For purposes of this exercise, let's call emailing, texting and IM-ing solitary activities. Even though they involve other people, they are still done in others' absence.)

Solitary activities at work primarily involve writing, reading and analysis. This could include reading a contract very carefully, researching and studying information on the web, analyzing processes or documenting systems. Whichever you prefer – and you may actually enjoy all – there is no right answer. People tend to lean toward being more social or more solitary in their work activities. The important thing is that you know where your preferences lie.

SEDENTARY VS. ACTIVE

Almost all jobs that are performed in an office environment are primarily sedentary. The main forms of communication used in the workplace are email, IM and the telephone. None of these involve lifting your butt out of your chair. There are, however, office jobs that do involve more movement. You can spend your day visiting clients, for example, or you can stand in front of a classroom conducting trainings. If you are not necessarily committed to office work, you can spend your entire day on your feet. You can, for example, be a tour guide, a coach for a sports team, a yoga instructor or a police officer. Again, the question is: What is tolerable to *you*? How much time each day do you want to be sitting in front of a computer vs. moving around?

ANALYTIC VS. CREATIVE is something of a false dichotomy. Some analytic work can be creative in its own way (computer programming, for example) and creative work often requires a lot of analysis (such as interior design). What I'm trying to get at with this distinction is the idea that some work is reflective in nature and its primary output is the documentation of the reflection itself.

Reading a contract carefully and providing suggestions about how to improve it would, in this case, be an analytic activity. By contrast, a primarily creative job involves generating something that may not have existed before. Developing a new menu for a restaurant may be more of a creative act while reviewing the menu to document the nutritional value of each menu item may be more of an analytic act. Analytic work tends to be *advisory* in nature. You may be identifying risks, understanding data and making recommendations. Creative work is *constructive* in nature. You may be describing new product specifications, delivering services or writing a novel. In simple (and, perhaps, reductionist) terms, analytic jobs are for thinkers, creative jobs are for do-ers.

FOCUSED VS. VARIED

The frequent mention of multi-tasking as an important job skill is an indicator that many jobs today involve a high degree of variation. You may be answering an email, switch to a phone call, switch back to your email and then IM someone to ask them a question. Your work day may involve the furthering of numerous activities that involve various aspects of your job responsibilities. Customer service positions are an example of this. In a customer-facing role, you might deal with several different customer concerns each day that require communication and follow-up with many different parties. Sales is another role that involves incremental work on many different fronts each day.

A more focused job position, by contrast, may involve some amount of communication, but is primarily focused on one major deliverable at a time. For example, a software developer may attend meetings and read specifications, but their primary focus each day is on writing code for a specific project with a known deadline. Another example of a focused job position is a market research analyst who spends his or her day reviewing and summarizing data for a specific assignment.

For each of these dimensions, consider how much time you would like to spend, on average, each day. For example, you might say "For the Group vs. Solitary dimension, I would like to spend 20% of my day talking to people and 80% of my day working at my computer." Complete the following table to document your preferences.

For this dimension...	...I would like to spend my day in the following way:
Group vs. Solitary	
Sedentary vs. Active	
Analytic vs. Creative	
Focused vs. Varied	

A conventional law firm job is *solitary*, *sedentary*, *analytic*, and *focused*. This doesn't describe every job in the legal profession; but if you are a corporate attorney in a large law firm, this is a fairly accurate characterization. Legal practice is *solitary* in nature because legal work is focused on billable hours. You bill for your time by sitting in front of your computer and conducting research, analysis, or writing. As such, the job is primarily a *sedentary* one. Time spent moving about from one place to another is generally not billable and, as such, is not a common feature of legal work. Practicing corporate law in a large firm is primarily *analytic* in nature. You spend your time reviewing the creative efforts of others. Your goal is to clean up the mess when accidents or disagreements happen, or to try to prevent bad things from happening in the first place. You spend more time on *focused* and billable activities, rather than moving from one activity to another.

If you want to pursue a legal job outside of working in a firm, you have a chance to vary from the norm. For example, a professional mediator's role is group-oriented, at least somewhat active, both analytic and creative and varied. If you work as an immigration attorney at a non-profit organization, you might spend your days conducting in-person consultations with your clients and creating legal guides that reflect the latest developments in immigration law. If you are a public defender, you will spend a good amount of your time interviewing your clients and deposing witnesses. If money is one of your primary motivators in considering law, it is worth noting that the more group-oriented, active, creative, and varied your job is, the less money you are likely to make (at least for the first five to ten years).

A great resource for gathering data in this area is talking to practicing attorneys. While you may not collect much new data from those working in corporate law, you will certainly get interesting insights from those working in government roles (such as a prosecutor, public defender, or an analyst for a government agency), public-interest positions (such as lawyers in political advocacy organizations), corporate counsel, or private practice. These positions may look a little different from the legal norm, as they are less likely to be centered on billable hours and provide more flexibility and variation.

To evaluate the legal profession as a candidate for your talent, review the preferences you documented in the table above and compare it to the data you have collected. If you want to spend at least half your day moving around and talking to people, a legal career might not be a good match. If you like focused study and careful analysis, law might be right up your alley.

STABILITY

How important is job stability to you? Job stability refers to the idea that your job is not sensitive to the economic environment. There are two aspects to this: First, your job is not likely to become *obsolete* or *off-shored*. For example, as the number of online travel-booking options has proliferated, the job of the travel agent has almost entirely become obsolete. A job that is off-shored is one that can be performed more cheaply overseas. The software industry, for example, has seen many programming jobs shifted to developing countries where talent is cheaper. A second aspect of job stability is the idea that a job role is essential regardless of the economic climate. For example, we may need just as many morticians, firefighters and physicians in good times as is necessary in times of economic recession.

Some people prefer high-stability jobs. This is particularly true for people who like to plan out their life's trajectory. They want to graduate from college or graduate school, get a job, get married, have kids, send their kids to college and retire with sufficient investments to support them in their old age. For this group, a stable job means that they will accomplish their life plans with minimal interruption or complication. They may gravitate to careers with established paths to promotion and pay scales. A job with the Federal government is an example of this. In government work, jobs, pay scales and pension plans are clearly defined. Depending on where someone works in the government, their job may be stable regardless of the overall economic climate. Another stable field is academics. Traditionally, teachers or professors have enjoyed a high level of stability in their careers. Once they gain tenure, they effectively have a job for life. For this group, knowing that they have a steady income today and will have a pension when they retire is more valuable than earning more money or being promoted.

Why would someone prefer a less stable job or career path? Oftentimes, the greater the risk involved in a job, the greater the reward. Entrepreneurs are an extreme in this case. When they start a new business, they could lose their entire investment or they could profit handsomely. Entrepreneurs typically value being the primary decision-maker in their business life and enjoy feeling like their fortunes will be made or lost through their own efforts. Entrepreneurs may also derive satisfaction from the process of growing a business from an idea to a successful and profitable enterprise.

Even if you aren't an entrepreneur, however, you may enjoy a career that is exposed to the dynamism of the marketplace. In highly–functioning companies, excellent employees are recognized and rewarded. Employees serve in particular job functions, but they are also free to stretch their abilities and take on new roles. They are judged and promoted based on their results. In this environment, someone who is bright, organized, flexible and personable will thrive. For example, Product Managers who manage particularly successful products will likely receive generous bonuses, stock options or grants and opportunities to take on new projects. They can guide their companies to take on new investments because the company respects their judgment. If they want to change roles in the future, the good will they have built within their firm will open doors to new opportunities. While a college professor may have more stability in their career, someone in the business world has more profit and flexibility.

Many people already know in their gut how important stability is to them. Pre-med students are classic cases of people who value stability. Medical training is essentially a ten-year investment and most people who are physicians remain in the health care profession for the rest of their lives. During their very first Human Biology class, they know that they are preparing for a life-long career that will last them until they retire. People who enjoy taking more risks will express themselves differently in college – they may not be sure what kind of job they want when they graduate, but they tend to be effective in whatever environment they are put in. They may take on part-time jobs or internships that give them the flavor of different work environments.

Determining your preference for stability is largely an intuitive task. If you don't already have a strong sense of risk aversion or if you haven't already defined what you want the rest of your life to look like, chances are that you don't *require* stability in your career path. You might like the idea of stability – most people would appreciate never having financial worries – but it is probably not an essential part of your personality. I can make this assertion confidently based on life experience – you simply don't meet many people who discover that they need a stable career path late in life. While risk preferences for some people change – for example, when they have kids – this is more of a circumstantial consideration rather than a foundational aspect of their personality. Most people occupy some kind of middle ground – they can tolerate a job in the business world and appreciate it when they get bonuses, raises or promotions. They would like to avoid being part of a layoff, but their sense of well-being isn't fundamentally shaken if they have to look for a new job.

If you have a strong need for stability, you should create success criteria around this. Is your ideal to hold a job at one company, university, or government agency for most of your working life? If an organization were recruiting you, would it be effective to tell you that you will get a full pension after twenty years on the job? Or are your success criteria more around the nature of the career path itself? For example, one might imagine that society will always need nurses and doctors, so the risk of high unemployment in the healthcare industry is unlikely. Try to determine what aspects of job stability are important to you and express them as success criteria. For example, you might want to say, "I want a job in a stable career that can pretty much guarantee me employment for the rest of my working life." Or, you might assert that, "I want a job with a pension plan that kicks in after fifteen years of continuous employment."

The legal career path is a stable one in certain respects, but it is highly sensitive to economic conditions. Let's consider its stability first. It is probably a true statement that our society will always need lawyers. In the United States, lawsuits are common, business is highly regulated and there is no lack of contracts that need to be negotiated. Legal practice in Western society, defined broadly, can be traced back to ancient Greece. There will be a need for lawyers far into the future, as long as civilized society exists.

Another thing that people like about a law degree is that once you pass the bar, you are unquestioningly qualified to do *something*. When many people graduate from college, they feel like they are all *potential* and no *experience*. They may even have a passion for a particular career path, but they don't know what to do in order to realize it. In a sense they are qualified to start *trying* anything, but bring no real credentials to the table. Potential employers have to take it on faith that they are ready to take on particular job responsibilities.

When graduating from law school, however, there is a well-established path for first-year legal associates. If you graduate from an ABA approved school and pass the bar exam, you are sufficiently prepared for the tasks of a starting associate. When law firms hire you, they know what they are getting and don't expect you to explain why you think you are qualified to take on a role in their field. This kind of certainty is a reassuring feeling for many people who decide to go to law school.

While the practice of law is not going anywhere, the availability of legal positions tends to expand and contract with the economy. In good times, law firms can't hire fast enough. Salaries and bonuses go up and law firms aggressively court new associates in their second and third years of law school. It's a great time to be a graduating law student and a lucrative time to be in the legal business. Partners in law firms get rich and their wealth trickles down to everyone who is billing their requisite number of hours at the firm.

In good times, law feels like a profoundly stable career. This is partly due to the system of law associate recruiting, particularly at top schools. In a good economy, recruiting new associates starts in the second year of law school. During the fall of your second year, on-campus recruiting begins. Law firms send representatives to schools to interview candidates for summer internship positions. Offers are made and, ideally, you leave the fall recruiting season with an internship offer in hand. From the law firm's perspective, they hope that you will enjoy your summer internship and start working for them after you graduate from law school. They will even cover the costs of your bar exam and bar prep course for you. What this means is that almost *two years* before you start working full-time for the firm, you already have a job offer. If you really like stability, it feels great knowing that – as long as you don't start failing your classes – you have a guaranteed job as soon as you graduate in twenty or so months.[8]

When bad times strike, however, legal practice feels just like any other career path. During the dot-com bust as well as the recent recession, graduating law students had their job offers rescinded, a particularly painful blow when they may have been thinking for the past eighteen months that their post-graduation employment had been locked in. Another symptom of poor economic times is that law firms start laying off their employees. For example, the *New York Times* reports the following about the current recession:

> *Just like investment banks, corporate law firms expanded their employee rolls during the boom, adding lawyers to practices that are now struggling. And these firms are now having to shrink their rosters in the face of diminishing profits.*
>
> *According to the Bureau of Labor Statistics, 5,500 jobs — for lawyers and staff positions like paralegals and clerks — were cut from the legal sector in January and February [2009].*[9]

In addition to shrinking staff rosters, many law firms have closed permanently. In San Francisco, for example, two respected firms, Thelen and Heller Ehrman closed for good, leaving hundreds of lawyers without jobs.[10] None of this is to say that law is *uniquely* impacted by economic downturns. Rather, it is simply to say that law is not *immune* to these downturns. While our society may always need lawyers, we need far fewer of them when the economy is bad.

8 To paint a completely accurate picture, the above description is what happens if you attend a top-five or top-ten law school. If your law school doesn't rank highly, you will have to work harder to secure your second-year summer internship. In any case, this will be easier when the overall economy is doing well.

9 See "The Legal Profession Feels the Pain of the Recession" – http://www.nytimes.com/2009/03/26/business/26law.html?_r=1&scp=1&sq=thelen&st=cse.

10 American Lawyer has been tracking law firm layoffs at top U.S. firms during the recent recession. See "The Layoff List" at http://www.law.com/jsp/tal/PubArticleTAL.jsp?id=1202425647706.

In specific ways, bad economic times hit attorneys harder than people in other professions. Because attorneys have specialized knowledge and work experience, they are less equipped to handle conditions where their talents are no longer needed. Lacking generalized business experience, it may be harder for them to look for roles in different industries or job functions. By contrast, someone with a background in sales could look for a sales position in another industry or try to find a position in marketing, advertising, or related areas. In addition, attorneys may still have law school debt that they need to service, so it is difficult to take on short-term positions that pay much less. Finally, many in law value the stability that legal practice has provided and find it excruciatingly difficult to ride out uncertain economic times.

If stability is very important for you, it's time to evaluate whether or not the legal profession is a good fit. In addition to the information presented here, it may be useful to do more web-based research and informational interviews to better understand whether or not the legal profession meets your success criteria. If you are looking for pension plans and an industry that is shielded from economic contraction, corporate law might not be the industry for you. You may consider legal positions in the Federal government that are considered more resistant to economic change. If that is your preference, be sure to interview attorneys who hold those jobs currently to better understand their sense of job stability.

CHAPTER THREE

THE LAW SCHOOL BAKE-OFF

Once you have identified the aspects of career that are important to you, described success criteria, gathered data and evaluated legal practice, you will come to one of three conclusions:

1. Legal practice meets all or most of my success criteria.
2. Legal practice meets some of my success criteria and fails on other counts.
3. Legal practice fails all or most of my success criteria.

If the legal profession fails to address all or nearly all of your career requirements, it's safe to say that law school is a "no-go" for you. If you still have a lingering feeling inside that you aren't ready to give up the idea of going to law school, it will be useful for you to read the remainder of this guide until your analysis and your gut instincts are in alignment.

If legal practice meets all or many of your success criteria, *it still doesn't mean that you should go to law school.* This may come as a surprise, but what we have been doing up to this point is seeing if law should be eliminated from the running altogether. If law seems like a *potentially* viable career path to you, you must now compare it to other career paths that also meet your success criteria.

Law may have proven itself to be worth investigation, but now it must differentiate itself from other career paths to prove that it is worth pursuing single-mindedly. Because law school is a three-year investment that costs tens- or hundreds-of-thousands of dollars, you must ask yourself: "If I make a similar investment of time and money, could I find an alternate career path that addresses my success criteria more fully, at less cost or with less risk?"

Realistically, few people are going to investigate this question comprehensively. There are so many potential career paths out there, you may not want to invest your time in understanding them and evaluating them across the dimensions we have identified. So, what are the shortcuts? What you need to do is generate options for yourself in a very focused way. Think of yourself as being on a treasure hunt where your goal is to locate the hidden career paths that will address your success criteria more effectively than law. Anything that doesn't come close to meeting your success criteria should be ignored. Ask yourself, for example, "How can I meet my success criteria in a job that doesn't require paying for three years of law school? Is there a way that I can work for three years instead of going to school for three years and end up with more of my success criteria met?"

To do this right, you need to start generating options. This is where many people give up. They decide that it is too much work to find alternative careers and if law school at least gets a passing grade, that's good enough. But here's what makes this step easier than you might think: At this stage of the game, we are doing a purely *practical* analysis. We aren't trying to figure out what your passion is in life or what your ideal career is. We aren't trying to determine how to map the things you enjoy on to a rewarding vocation. All we are trying to do is find something – *anything* – better than the law school option. That's what the Law School Bake-Off is all about. Can we find *any* career path that addresses your success criteria more completely or with less investment than law school? If so, law school loses; if not, law school wins.[11]

To generate options, the best place to start is your college career office. Make an appointment with one of the career advisors and bring your success criteria with you.[12]

11 For some people, this analytic approach is incomplete. What if, for example, being an actuary meets the same success criteria as law but requires less investment of time and money? According to the rules of the bake-off, being and actuary wins and being an attorney loses. But – if you think being an actuary is less interesting than being a lawyer, that's an important consideration. You have two options at this point: You can revisit your career attributes and add a new dimension; for example, "subject-matter interest." You can define success criteria for this attribute and compare the legal profession to other professions. Alternatively, you can wait until Part Two to think more about your personality and how it factors into your decision on whether or not to go to law school.

12 Note that if you have already graduated, you may still have access to your undergraduate college career office. Check with them directly before you assume that you are not entitled to access their resources. You might also check with your school's alumni office to see if they provide career counseling services or other resources. If both of these options are dead ends, I suggest working with a career coach who can help you think through these considerations.

Tell your career advisor, for example, "I need to generate a list of careers that can pay at least $80,000 per year, require no more than 50% of my time be spent in front of a computer, and involve varied activities that can be both analytic and creative." If your career advisor knows what they are doing, they can help you brainstorm or point you to other resources that will help you create a list.

This should be an easy need for your career office to fill. If, for some reason, you have a particularly poor career office or your career advisor is not helpful, find real people practicing in the business world to talk to. To find these real people, you can do anything from speaking to your friends' parents to asking your alumni association to help you find contacts. To help you brainstorm, almost anyone with at least five years' experience in the business world can help you. It's useful if their careers have some overlap with your success criteria, but it's not essential. The goal here is to find someone with more work experience than you who can help you with your list.

Another approach is to find people who graduated three to five years ago and conduct informational interviews with them. These should be people whose jobs at least somewhat meet your success criteria. Alternatively, they could be in career paths that *ultimately* lead to jobs that meet your success criteria. Talk to them about what you are looking for and brainstorm ideas with them. In addition to building up your list of career alternatives, get a sense for what their current lives are like. Pretend that instead of going to law school, they decided to pursue their current career. They have an income and real work experience by this time and will give you a sense of one possible path for your life.

Regarding income, keep in mind that you will likely graduate from law school with some amount of law school debt. If none of your interviewees are making the amount of money that you could make when you graduate from law school, remember that they have gotten to their current position without taking on any debt. Moreover, they have been earning a real income over the past number of years rather than living as a student. Given that, you should find out whether or not it is *ever* possible for someone in their career path to make the amount of money that you want to make.

Finally, there is our old friend the Internet. Use the Internet to help generate career alternatives by searching for job-oriented content that relates to your success criteria. Your career office should be able to provide you with good job-related web sites or databases. While web-based resources are good, don't use them as your primary area of research. Talking to career advisors and working professionals will be far more fruitful and will have the benefit of helping you build your professional network.

Once you have a list of potential alternatives to legal careers, take a few of them and start drilling down. Again, this is where web-based research and informational interviews will really help you. Remember, you aren't trying to figure out your ideal career at this point, you are just trying to get a decent list of 5-10 career options that might fare well against your success criteria. The goal is to analyze these career paths to see how they measure up against the legal profession.

It may be useful to make a table like the following one and start filling in the blanks. I've populated the table with some sample data (all completely made up), but you should use your own success criteria and career-oriented data for both the legal profession and your alternate careers. Note that my data points are primarily qualitative – I add comments to each cell to elaborate on the level of match. But you could also use a more quantitative system, for example using "Low," "Medium," or "High" to indicate how strongly each career path addresses your success criteria.

Criteria	Law	Sales	Fitness Instructor	Marketing
Make at least $80,000 per year.	Possible immediately after graduation from my chosen law school in three years.	Possible within 1-3 years, depending on the industry.	Could be possible if I start my own business. Haven't heard of any fitness instructors who make this much money.	Possible within 5 years.
Work no more than 50 hours per week.	I have a 50% chance of realizing this goal and also making the salary I want to make.	Typical. Could require more work in difficult industries.	Easily accomplished.	This is typical.
Work at a desk no more than 50% of the time.	Not very likely.	Possible. I could work in a sales position that involves meeting with clients at various locations.	Easily accomplished.	Maybe a 50-50 chance here. I could spend a lot of time talking to people and working in meetings. But there is also a lot of time spent at the desk.
Have a job that provides an average level of stability.	Easily accomplished.	Varies significantly based on industry and compensation structure.	Always busy during good times. People tend to stop paying for classes when the economy is in decline.	Easily accomplished.

In this imagined case, law is not a leader. All of the other careers are at least comparable in meeting the success criteria and none of the other careers require the same level of investment as a law degree. For this particular profile, the alternate career paths seem to provide better options.

Once you have the results of the bake-off, you will know if law is the perfect career path for meeting your success criteria. If you find no other career path that will meet your success criteria as fully or inexpensively as law, going to law school may be a great idea. If you find one or more career paths that meet your success criteria more fully or more inexpensively than law, law school is not a good idea (at least from a purely rational perspective).

A final note on this topic: I've mentioned the idea that law school requires an investment of time and money. While this is true, it could be argued that other career paths also require an investment of time and money in order to reach the required threshold for the success criteria. In the table above for example, I asserted that a marketer can make $80,000 within five years. Isn't it reasonable to assert that marketing, then, requires a five-year investment while law school only is a three-year investment? The missing piece in that assertion is the fact that law school costs money in two ways: First, your tuition, books, living expenses, and debt service are real money that you must pay as part of your investment. Second, in a marketing role, you receive a *salary* between now and the day you start earning $80,000. You might think of your early jobs in the marketing career path as paid training. By contrast, in law school, you pay to be trained.[13]

CODA: PURSUING LAW FOR A NON-LEGAL CAREER

I conclude this chapter with a brief note on an outlying case: Pursuing a law degree as a prerequisite for a non-legal career. Some people want a law degree to add status and credibility to their role in a non-legal career path. For example, if you want to be a politician or political advisor, a law degree might influence people's impression of you. Your law credential provides a badge of honor that enhances your esteem in others' eyes. Is it worth going to law school for this reason? There is no easily generalizable answer to this question. I would encourage you to re-read the ROI section of this document to find out if your investment is worth it. I also encourage you to investigate career paths that may provide more explicit preparation for public service, such as serving on committees of political parties or working in almost any role that gives you exposure to the political process. Finally, I suggest you talk to people in your field with and without law degrees and learn from their perspectives.

13 See the ROI discussion in this guide for more analysis of the costs of law school.

If you are pursuing a law degree because you think it will be good preparation for the business world, I would strongly encourage you to reconsider. In almost all cases, the business world values experience and results over education. An MBA is the only degree that has caché in the business world and, even then, it is not required for most positions. Further, lawyers are often perceived as lacking skills that are essential for business – risk-taking, dealing with uncertainty and decision-making under conditions of imperfect information. While a law degree is an interesting adjunct to a business career, I would generally not consider it helpful.

We can make decisions with greater speed and accuracy when we deeply understand our needs and desires.

PART TWO

KNOWING WHAT YOU WANT

I began the introduction to this book with a controversial assertion: Many people know, either consciously or unconsciously, what they should do, but aren't entirely satisfied with the conclusion they have reached. Some will look at the various financial and lifestyle trade-offs involved in legal education and practice and come to the conclusion that they should not attend law school. And yet, these same people might feel the possibility of attending law school continues to gnaw at them and they are unwilling to stop ruminating over the possibility. Alternatively, you may have decided to go to law school – you may even have been accepted to your first-choice law school – but you feel no passion or clarity about your decision to become an attorney. Why is this? Why are we left with decisions that feel incomplete or only half make sense?

CHAPTER FOUR

NO TURNING BACK

Before we explore the answers to these questions, I need to dispel one myth that causes many people to go to law school and stay in law school, even if they are not completely satisfied or committed. This myth can be devastating if it is part of your decision-making processes, and it will cause you to make harmful decisions over and over again. I call it the "no turning back" myth. Depending on where you are currently at in your process, you may be completing your law school applications, waiting for admission offers or simply waiting for school to start. You may have told your friends and family that you are going to law school; you may have asked your professors for letters of recommendation; you may have spent a considerable amount of money on the LSAT and application fees. At this point, you might feel like you've constructed an identity around being a future attorney and there is no turning back. You have announced this identity to many people and changing your mind will make you seem indecisive, fickle or not as "together" as you would like to have people see you. Alternatively, you may have told your friends and family that you are *not* going to law school and they all feel relieved that you won't be moving away, you won't be less available as a friend or partner and you won't be taking on a new identity that might feel threatening or intimidating to them. You may feel like changing your mind will disrupt them and create unwelcome repercussions for you in your relationships.

In his classic book (you may have even read it in your business or psychology classes) *Influence – Science and Practice*, Robert Cialdini describes "commitment and consistency" as a tactic that sales people and advertisers use to influence consumers. This sales tactic involves a salesperson or marketer presenting an abstract concept that elicits your agreement. For example, "Wouldn't you agree that a new car should protect you and your passengers from the top driving hazards?" Well, of course. Who wouldn't want a safe car? The sales person may then present a vehicle option that costs much more than you were intending to spend and address any objections you may have to the price by recalling the fact that you initially committed to the idea of wanting a safe car. Now, the state-of-the-art safety features may cost an additional $15,000, but you said that safety for yourself and your passengers was important, didn't you? Cialdini observed that people want to seem consistent and hate being called out on their inconsistencies. This makes us agree to things that we would normally not agree to. In his discussion of commitment and consistency, Cialdini concludes, "although consistency is generally good, even vital, there is a foolish, rigid variety that is to be shunned."

I am here to tell you that you can change your mind *completely* today. As an adult and as a human, you are entitled to take in new information, evaluate it and make different decisions. We are all evolving beings and our knowledge of the world, our understanding of ourselves and our ability to process this information grows and increases over time. If you think that your decisions may cause harm to others or maybe some embarrassment to yourself, those impacts are *minor* in comparison to the harm you cause yourself by living a life that is less than what you deserve. Additionally, you are not responsible for other people's emotional reactions to the decisions that you make in your life. No one has to live your life except you and it is unfair and unreasonable for anyone to make you responsible for their happiness or sense of identity.

You may be embarrassed about changing your mind or you may simply feel dread about having to communicate with so many people about your changed decision. These are understandable feelings; but, avoiding these feelings by moving forward with a bad decision – a decision you know is wrong – is a terrible choice. I suggest that you devise some strategies to help disseminate your new decision to everyone who you would like to tell. This involves a broadcasting strategy – such as an email or a series of phone calls or in-person conversations – as well as a message, i.e. a simple description of your new direction and, if you choose, a brief rationale for your decision. Whenever possible, get help from a close friend or family member who can help communicate your change of heart while minimizing any possible negative repercussions on yourself.

Just to make sure I've been completely clear, I'll mention a few more points. You have the right to change your mind, even if:

> Your parents really want you to go to law school and have their self-esteem wound up in your decision.
>
> Your professors wrote you glowing letters of recommendation in order to support your law school application.
>
> All of your friends are applying to law/business/medical school.
>
> Your grandma gave you a $500 check to help you pay for application fees.
>
> You aced the LSAT.

Or...

> You told all of your friends that lawyers are scoundrels and that you would never "sell out."
>
> You just started a new job.
>
> You told your girlfriend or boyfriend that you wouldn't move to another city.
>
> Your friends threw a great big party for you to celebrate your decision to not go in to law.

None of these points or any of their near cousins should influence your decision to attend or not attend law school. To reiterate, this is *your* life and you are *entitled* to make the best decision for yourself today. Your friends, family, co-workers, etc. are all adults and are capable of handling whatever disappointment or confusion they experience when they take in new information. And if they aren't capable, it is not your role to be their caretaker.

The decision to make a new decision feels fraught because a) it affects your self-image and b) it relies on the ability of others to take in and process new information. Let's consider these points one-by-one.

First, your self-image. You might feel that because you have publicly and decisively announced your intention to go to law school, you will look silly if you suddenly change your mind with an equal amount of publicity and decisiveness. Maybe you want to seem consistent, as discussed above. Or maybe you are just embarrassed about seeming like you don't have all of the answers or don't have your act together. If it troubles you to have your peers, friends, family or mentors witness the flux and evolution of your decision-making process, it is time to cut yourself some slack. No one has all of the answers in life and thoughtful people can hold opinions that are diametrically opposed to what they previously believed. We are *thinking beings* and are capable of taking in new information and making decisions based on that information. As someone once said, we are all students in life, still learning life's lessons. If it hurts too much or feels too frightening to have people witness your indecision or vacillation, I encourage you to consider that there is more to you than your need for approval and your fear of social rejection. Those that are close to you will understand that you are an evolving personality and they will appreciate the thoughtfulness and passion that you bring to your life's decisions. If there is no one in your life who can be interested in and supportive of you in this way, it is time to build new relationships that foster the fullness of who you are.

If you have a strong fear of disappointing people and that is what blocks you from making a positive life change for yourself, it is time for you to set healthy relationship boundaries and cultivate trust in the resiliency of those around you. Setting healthy boundaries means that you acknowledge and feel deeply that your life decisions are truly your own. Your decisions may surprise, confuse, delight, or disappoint others; but their reaction to your decisions is not your responsibility. It is theirs. Trusting in the resilience of others means acknowledging that other people can experience disappointment, surprise, or fear about your decisions, but – in simple terms– they will get over it. If they truly care about you, they will experience their reaction, take responsibility for it and, eventually, support you in your new life direction. [14]

14 As additional food for thought, consider a 2009 study by Lexis-Nexis that found 20% of law school students regretted their decision to attend law school. That's one in five law students who have accumulated debt and missed out on other career opportunities because they didn't take the time or have the courage to consider their law school decision carefully. See http://thelawschooldecision.com/2010/02/27/law-school-waiting-game-as-a-chance-to-re-group/ and http://legalblogwatch.typepad.com/legal_blog_watch/2009/12/firms-clients-differ-on-legal-industrys-forecast.html.

CHAPTER FIVE

DECISIONS THAT MAKE SENSE AND FEEL RIGHT

Have you ever made a decision that both made sense and felt right? For many people, the answer is "no," and there is no shame in this. Strangely, I think, decision-making curriculum is almost completely absent in primary or secondary education. Young people are sometimes encouraged to make good decisions – "study hard," "don't use drugs," "eat healthy" – but these are less *decisions* than *directives* that they are supposed to follow. These injunctions, provided by the adult world, are directives to be obeyed rather than understood. We often aren't told why or how to conform to the guidance we are given, and we are even less frequently told how to develop our *own* internal goals, guidelines, and processes.

In fact, our education system leaves many people in the position of never making major life decisions on their own. It is a common profile of a first year law student to have made good grades in high school, attended a competitive college (and excelled) and then applied to law school in the interest of becoming a lawyer. In the entire process, they followed the guidance of others ("get good grades") and were only once empowered to make a significant life decision on their own. Typically this decision is to choose a major in college. Of course, law school doesn't favor any particular college major, so this decision is in many ways irrelevant. In their second year in law school, they will get an internship at a law firm, which will then hire them after they graduate. They will then become lawyers and work hard in order to pay off their law school debts. Somewhere along the way, they may get involved in a long-term relationship and possibly have children. While this path does, in fact, include many major decisions, in another light, it affords few opportunities to think critically about one's life goals and deepest desires. You could say that it addresses one desire completely – that of social compliance and risk-avoidance – and others not at all.

None of this is to say that it is bad to get good grades, to get a professional degree or to have a challenging job. And it's certainly not to say that it is a bad thing to be in a relationship and to have children if that is your desire. My point is that simple compliance to the directives of our parents, teachers and peers does not equal decision-making prowess. We have created a culture where, if we let it happen, every decision is already made for us. Decisions don't necessarily feel right or wrong; they are, in fact, scarcely analyzed and primarily make sense because they reflect a social consensus (i.e. that is what you are supposed to do).

One reason why people make bad decisions or inconsistently make good decisions is that they have no framework for analyzing their circumstances.

I began this section by saying there is no shame in never having made a decision that both makes sense and feels right. We are raised to have decisions made for us, regardless of how those decisions feel or whether they account for our current circumstances. As children, we *need* to have decisions made for us. Ideally our parents protect us from harm and provide us with guidance based on their experience. As adults, we must cultivate our *own* inner system for understanding ourselves and our priorities. We need to learn to measure our circumstances and follow a path, even if it is an uncommon one. We need to learn how to know what data to look for, what guidance to follow and what opinions to ignore.

Why is it important that a decision both make sense and feel right? When a decision makes sense, it means that you have taken an honest, dispassionate look at the data available to you and you have analyzed this data with the appropriate tools. Part One of this guide provides tools that lead you to a sensible answer to your law school decision. The process of making sense of your circumstances is an *evolving* one and requires an *honest* look at the relevant information. I emphasize honesty here, because it is important to consider data that is both favorable and unfavorable to your underlying desires. Looking at a decision with this kind of objectivity gives you a sense of confidence that you have mastered all of the variables available to you.

In almost every circumstance, you will be making a decision based on incomplete information. Even if you could understand all of the information available to you in the present, you have only a limited ability to accurately conjecture about the future. Will you win the lottery? Get hit by a train? No one can know these things for sure. One way to address the uncertainty is to make use of tools. I've introduced a number of these tools in the previous chapters and everyone should have a few of them in their life's tool kit.

One reason why people make bad decisions or inconsistently make good decisions is that they have no *framework* for analyzing their circumstances. A framework is a set of rules or exercises that can be repeated and applied to many different circumstances to aid you in finding answers to difficult questions. There are many decision analysis frameworks out there and I encourage you to investigate them if you are interested. They will provide structure for you whenever you face life's challenges, and will help you stay lucid, even in times of stress.[15]

We can make decisions with greater speed and accuracy when we deeply understand our needs and desires. Self-knowledge provides an inherent framework for guiding our life decisions and for keeping our actions in alignment with our life's purpose. Self-knowledge is more than just knowing what we want; it is knowing *why* we want what we want and what parts of our personality are being served by our choices. We will look at this more deeply; but for now, I just want to focus on the fact that self-knowledge gives you an edge in your ability to make good decisions and make them quickly.

Self-knowledge can simply be rules of thumb about what you want from your life, what your temperament is and what your needs are. It can also be a *felt* sense of what

15 If you are interested in a terrific, accessible and profoundly rational framework for decision-making, I strongly encourage you to pick up a copy of Smart Choices: A Practical Guide to Making Better Life Decisions by Hammond, Keeny and Raiffa. Read the reviews on Amazon if you are interested in learning more: http://www.amazon.com/gp/product/0767908864?ie=UTF8&tag=lawschooldecision-20&linkCode=as2&camp=1789&creative=390957&creativeASIN=0767908864.

serves you emotionally and what is harmful to your well-being. Some people have a gut sense of who they are that is so strong and so honest that they tend to have a good feeling or bad feeling about their life circumstances and the options before them. To whatever degree your sense of self is refined, it will generally mean that you can spend less time analyzing a problem and more time directing yourself to a solution.

By analogy, consider what a CEO needs to know in order to run a successful business. Minimally, a CEO's job is to generate profit for the company and to increase shareholder value. For a CEO, this is an obvious fact. When decisions have to be made, the CEO can scrutinize them under the lens of this directive – maximizing profit and shareholder value – and determine the proper course to take. Of course, a CEO's decisions are generally more sophisticated than this; but the bottom line is that if an idea does not increase shareholder value in the short term or the long term, it is typically rejected. Now, imagine a CEO's job if he or she didn't realize that the primary goal in business is to maximize profit? How would they make decisions? It's hard to imagine, isn't it? How would you run a business if you didn't realize that your goal was to make money? How would you react to the challenges that you were confronted with and the questions you were asked each day? It would probably be confusing and possibly terrifying.

Many people live their lives like our confused CEO. That is to say that many people live their lives not knowing fundamentally what they are about and what is important to them. They don't know how to consistently make good decisions because they don't understand why one option would serve them more or less than another. I'm not just talking here about understanding what serves you best financially or otherwise materially. I'm talking about what serves you as a human being in the deepest parts of your personality. In your life, I wish for you that you understand yourself with sufficient depth that you are crystal clear in your decisions and feel empowered and affirmed by the choices you make. My desire is that you create a life that touches you deeply and gives you the freedom to express your wholeness. As a conscious being you are comprised of memories, feelings and capacities that should all be integrated and expressed as part of your life's path. And it just so happens that experiencing yourself as a whole person, as aware and realized as you can be at this point in your life, will make you an incredible and efficient decision–maker.

GETTING TO KNOW YOURSELF

Gaining self-knowledge is a life's journey. Our minds and our hearts are constantly evolving as a result of new experiences. As we move forward in life's journey, we process our experiences and increase our capacity to understand our lives and take resourceful action. In your own life, you can see how your experience has fueled your growth and your ability to handle life's challenges. We move from being infants, entirely dependent on our parents for physical sustenance and emotional nurturing, to being highly functioning adults. Along the way, if we are lucky, we have internalized the care-taking our parents provided us as children. We carry a sense of safety, self-care and emotional confidence into our interactions with our friends, teachers, lovers, landlords and the DMV. Simply put, our parents' love, emotional resiliency and competence as caregivers allow us to develop the capacity to care for ourselves.

Developing self-knowledge continues far beyond the eighteen years we spend in our parents' care. As a result, gaining self-knowledge is not a one-time event. It is an ongoing effort and an approximate one at best. Because we constantly grow as people, our deepest needs are a moving target.

To make things even more interesting (and ambiguous), we unconsciously throttle how much and how quickly self-knowledge is integrated into our conscious awareness. This is a significant point and is worth your consideration. I'll repeat it here:

We unconsciously throttle how much and how quickly self-knowledge is integrated into our conscious awareness.

This means that we are not always *ready* to really take in all of the information that is available to us. Our psyche tries to protect us from information that we are not yet prepared to face. Unfortunately, this includes knowledge about our needs that, for some reason, is profoundly uncomfortable for us to look at directly and honestly.

This is somewhat complicated, so I'll break it down to make sure it's clear what I'm getting at. First is the idea that we are not conscious of all of our motivations at any given moment. Some people may object to the idea that there are unconscious impulses guiding their behavior; but on closer inspection, there are many ways that this occurs in our day-to-day lives. Have you ever started getting a little hungry, but not realized your hunger until you were completely ravenous? Have you ever felt irritable or unhappy and then realized that you didn't get enough sleep the previous night? Have you ever felt "off" – maybe grumpy or sad – and then realized that a contentious conversation you had earlier in the day was still bothering you? Have you ever needed to study for an exam that you dread, but a dozen small things– answering a phone call, going to the gym, responding to an email or backing up your hard drive – all prevent you from getting started? In all of these examples, you have needs that, for one reason or another, do not bubble up into your consciousness. There's nothing to be embarrassed about by this; it's simply how everyone's mind works.

I mentioned some day-to-day examples, but this same mechanism is at play in the bigger decisions in our lives. For example, people make decisions every day in order to conform to social expectations. They do this, even when the consequences of their behaviors are extremely dangerous to themselves or others. Every day, people vandalize, steal or start unhealthy drug habits because they are in a social milieu that encourages or even requires that behavior. Their unconscious need may be to hold on to a sense of belonging or gain a sense of purpose or self-esteem. We call this "peer pressure" and its influence is strong because we are hard-wired to fit in and to seek social approbation. Another example: People spend large amounts of money on luxury goods not simply because they are fun, high quality or unique. Luxury goods are popular because they confer status on their owners and may help manage deeper feelings of insecurity or a need for attention. Peer pressure and status-seeking are not necessarily bad; that's not the point. The point is that these are examples of unconscious behaviors that drive life decisions. It's important to be as aware as we can of these unconscious motivations so we can make choices with a clearer head.

Part of the challenge of cultivating self-knowledge is that our desires are often unconscious. Now, let's consider the second part of this problem, the idea that we throttle how much and how quickly we surface information from our unconscious. If it were possible for us to choose complete self-awareness, such that all of our unconscious memories, feelings and capacities would immediately come in to view, it would be easy to understand ourselves and it would be simpler to make big decisions in life. And yet, summoning this clarity is not a simple act of will. Our minds are extremely sophisticated organs that have been trained unconsciously for our entire lives to organize our awareness in a way that supports our safety and comfort. For our minds to surface memories or desires from our unconscious that are uncomfortable, we need to have a sufficient sense of safety that we can respond to the new information with resilience.

For example, if your parents have always given you great praise for your academic achievement, even *thinking* about not going to law school may be too painful for you. Unless you feel safe enough about your capacity to succeed in life through your own efforts, you may not even acknowledge or consider the possibility of making life choices that would disappoint your parents. Because your relationship with your parents (and, hence, your safety) seems easily imperiled, your mind may not even expose to you to the fact that your choices are driven by your need for their approval and your fear of rejection.

Another example involves the way we handle our self-image in the face of deep insecurities. Maybe you went to college in your hometown or in a nearby city where you were surrounded by familiar faces or, at least, familiar geography. Going to law school may involve traveling to another state that you've never been to and being surrounded by completely new people who may be much smarter/more accomplished/more together than you are. This experience may be new to you and you may be frightened; but you may tell yourself "law school isn't right" for you, you "wouldn't be happy as a lawyer" or "it's too expensive."

We hide from our true feelings because, at this stage of our maturation, certain aspects of our truth are too frightening for us to handle. Our mind is working in the interest of our safety and comfort, so it works hard to shield us from information that will undermine our sense of stability. Ironically, our minds sometimes prefer painful situations because, in their own way, they feel safer than facing the underlying problems that keep us stuck. What I have said is true of people, regardless of age, education, gender or any other factor you can imagine. Our minds will only tell us what we are ready to hear. When you deepen your knowledge of yourself, you are asking your unconscious mind to take a risk and stretch the boundaries of what feels safe. And your unconscious mind does not always cooperate.

Another way to think about this is through an athletic metaphor. Imagine that for eighteen years of your life, you were taught to hold a tennis racket in your right hand. Every time you played tennis, you played with your right hand and you ended up having a reasonable amount of success as a tennis player as a result. At some point in time, you stopped having to think about which hand to hold the racket in. It just felt natural to pick up a tennis racket with your right hand. If you were asked "Why do you play tennis with your right hand?", you might say "it feels natural" or "it's the way you are supposed to play" or "it's the only way that makes sense." But you might not think to say "it's how I was taught," "I've practiced this way for eighteen years," or "I never thought about trying my left hand." Now, if a major research study came out that showed that playing tennis with your left hand produces much better results, how would you react? Would you ignore the report and pretend it didn't exist? Would you decide that something had to be wrong with the study because it "doesn't make sense" to play with anything but your right hand? Would you decide that switching hands is too hard? Even if you decided to start playing with your left hand, you would not see improvement overnight. You simply can't overcome eighteen years of practice in one day.

Both our conscious and unconscious minds work in this way. They have practiced and become good at certain skills over the many years that you have been alive. You have been exposed to a variety of environmental influences (your parents, your economic situation, your health, etc.) and you have learned to cope with the stresses and joys of being alive. Many of those coping skills were taught to you in your family or in your schools. Some skills you figured out on your own based on your brain's sense of the best response at a particular moment in your emotional development. If you have faced trauma in your life, you may have experienced accelerated and intense learning in order to deal with the overwhelming (and often terribly unjust) circumstances to which you have been subjected. Whatever life skills you have developed, you have likely practiced them for many years, and your habits and thought processes – even the ones that are causing you great suffering – will not go down without a fight.

To understand and identify your underlying motivations requires a great deal of honesty. Honesty is a difficult but essential skill to develop when navigating the forks in the road of your life's journey. A willingness to be honest is a signal to your unconscious mind that you are ready to receive more information. When your unconscious mind yields new insights, it may feel painful, relieving or a little bit of both.

A complete discussion of cultivating self-awareness exceeds the scope of this book. There are many paths, and you must choose one that is right for you. This could include talking to friends, learning to trust your gut instincts or speaking with a career counselor. It could also include meditation, journaling or therapy. For the purposes of this guide, I will focus on two points in particular: the Five Naked Truths and Understanding Your Potential.

CHAPTER SIX

THE FIVE NAKED TRUTHS

What I call the "Five Naked Truths" are five honest, but sometimes embarrassing or hard–to–admit reasons why people go to law school. In this section, I'm putting all of my cards on the table and sharing with you what drove me to attend a top-tier law school. I was originally planning on calling this section the Five Ugly Truths; but, in fact, there is nothing ugly about these motivations. I wouldn't even characterize them as "Bad Reasons to Attend Law School." They are simply human desires that it is important to be honest about. I was only partially cognizant of each of these truths before I started law school and have only become fully aware of my true motivations long after the fact.

At the end of each truth, I will ask you a series of questions. I suggest that you take a moment to reflect on these questions as you read them and to pledge to yourself to answer them with as much honesty as is available to you.

A final note, which I will attempt to reiterate in my discussion of each of these truths, is that I do not believe that everyone in law school goes there because of these motivations. I also don't believe that you should only go to law school if you are somehow perfectly "pure" in your intentions. I'm also not asking you to change your personality in some way to conform to a perfect law school student profile.

What I am doing is just asking you to take a moment, perhaps many moments, to think carefully about why you really want to go to law school. Whether or not you decide to go to law school, you will be a better decision–maker in your life if you know yourself as clearly as possible.

THE FIRST TRUTH: STATUS

Some people go to law school to gain status. Status in this sense could be personal or professional. Seeking personal status from being an attorney means that you believe others will hold you higher because you are a professional, attended a particular law school or have a career path that some equate with money, power or mental ability. It might be exciting to think about appending a "J.D." to your name as a way of announcing to the world that you have accomplished something difficult that they have not had the intelligence or tenacity to achieve. Professional status means that you believe that having a law degree will elevate your position in a non-law career, such as being a politician or working in civil service.

In some ways, you can accomplish both personal and professional status by becoming an attorney. Many people will indeed be impressed and even intimidated by your degree, particularly if you went to law school at Harvard, Stanford or Yale. We live in a status-oriented society. If your peacock feathers are bigger, brighter, and more colorful than the rest of the pack, someone is sure to notice. Lawyers have found great success in our society and we can all name a few of them, like Barack Obama, Sandra Day O'Connor, Johnnie Cochran, John Grisham and numerous CEOs of Fortune 1000 companies. Sounds pretty impressive, doesn't it?

There are two problems with the status game. The first is that there will always be someone who is smarter, luckier, richer and better looking than you are. This is particularly true in law school, where you will meet some of the smartest people you have ever met. Even if you are the smartest person in your class, there will be other law schools ranked higher than yours. And even if you are the smartest person from the top law school in the country, guess what? Some people profoundly dislike lawyers and think of legal practice as the lowest profession on Earth. They will think that you are narrow-minded, uncreative and, at best, a necessary evil in business that they would rather do without.

The second problem is the more significant one. If you seek out status to feel better about yourself, you are looking in the wrong direction. Having an identity as an attorney may prop up your ego to some degree, but it masks a deeply flawed and masochistic self-perception. In this book, first and foremost, I want to be on your side and I feel compelled to share with you a simple and profound truth: It is your *birthright* to feel comfortable being exactly as you are.

As a child, it is our parents' role to provide enough unconditional love that we can move into the world with a high sense of self-worth and an ability to take risks that help us express and expand who we are. If you do not feel at the core of your being that you can accept yourself exactly *as* you are and exactly *where* you are at this moment in your life, law school will do more to undermine your self-confidence than to buoy it. If being an attorney gives you a sense of self-worth, what will happen if you lose your job by being laid off or fired? Or what if you hate your job – the long hours, the repetitive tasks, the frustrating clients – but you can't bear to leave the legal profession because the very idea undermines a major pillar of your self-esteem?

When I entered law school, I was not a status seeker *per se*, but I was awash in insecurity. I had just completed my Ph.D. at Stanford, but I still felt like I hadn't proven myself. I was fortunate enough to get in to Stanford Law School thanks to a combination of my LSAT score, undergraduate GPA and my letters of recommendation. Getting a law degree at one of the top law schools in the country would certainly be enough to prove that I was indeed intelligent and worthy of respect. On top of that, I already had a Ph.D., which would certainly cause my law school peers to tremble in their shoes. I had played the status game and won.

Of course, when I started as a 1L (a first-year law student), one third of my cohort had advanced degrees. Ph.Ds. were numerous and those that held one didn't stand out in the way I had expected. Many of my colleagues were *breathtakingly* intelligent and I was humbled when I saw how their personalities and capacities were a perfect fit for law school. I still had some minor distinction – I was the only 1L who was training for a 50-mile marathon during the first semester of law school. In between study sessions, I would run up to twenty miles a day each weekend and was in excellent physical shape. It was clear to me that I needed to do this. I had already run in the San Francisco Marathon, but that was just a 26-mile marathon and heck, anyone could do that. But how many people do you know who have run a 50-mile marathon…

To be honest, going to law school at Stanford did aid my self-esteem in at least one way. As I made my way through law school, I found myself to have certain academic strengths and deficits, characteristics I found in most of my fellow students. When I saw people who far exceeded my academic abilities or interests, I was clear that I didn't want to be them. I simply couldn't get myself to generate a lot of hustle around a game that I didn't feel like playing and would probably never be among the best at. I could have worked harder and achieved more; but, ultimately, I realized that I didn't want to. Seeing that was comforting, because it focused me more on my own interests. I also saw that even the smartest, most accomplished people I had ever met still had human foibles and mundane life struggles. This was a valuable lesson and it was what I needed at the time.

If I had it all to live over today, I would ask myself – whether or not I decided to attend law school – to take the time to attend to the part of my personality that was in such desperate need to feel okay, to be accepted and to have the right to take up space in the world. I was not emotionally resourceful enough at the time to give myself the kind of attention that I so urgently needed.

To tell if your motivation to attend law school is driven by status, ask yourself the following questions:

- Are you going to law school to prove something to your friends, family, or yourself?
- If you do not pursue a professional degree or an advanced degree of some sort, will you still feel like you deserve personal and professional respect from yourself and others?
- How much does it matter to you that you attend a top-tier law school?
- Do you esteem people with professional degrees differently from people with non-professional degrees?
- In social situations, do you try to figure out how you rank in terms of education, athleticism, income, etc.?

THE SECOND TRUTH: PLEASING OTHERS

Some people apply to law school to please others, typically their parents. This can happen for a number of reasons, but a very common one is when your parents are also professionals of some sort. It is common for law to run in families and many people who go to law school have parents or grandparents who are or were attorneys. But a parent-pleasing motivation can also be present when a parent is a physician, professor or part of any other credentialed profession.

When professional degrees run in the family, there can be a lifelong expectation from your parents that you will minimally maintain the social or intellectual status of the family. Running off and starting a rock band would be frowned upon unless it was a last hurrah before starting as a 1L in a top-tier law school. You may have been raised with the sense that you would follow in your parents' footsteps. If you were fortunate to have your parents fund your undergraduate education, you may feel like you owe it to them to pursue a career of their choosing rather than your own.

Even if your parents weren't professionals or your undergraduate benefactors, they may have their self-esteem tied up in your achievement. They may orient their identities around having a daughter or son who has accomplished so much and is continuing their upward mobility. They may have used your accomplishments to gain social status with their friends and co-workers. They may have always wanted to do more in their own professional careers and see your attendance at law school as a way of realizing their own dreams. In all of this, they may tell you that they want the best for you or they want to prevent you from making bad decisions. But they may actually need you to shore up their never-fully-developed self-esteem, to restore their shattered dreams or realize their unexpressed potential. In this way, your parents may see you more as an extension of their own desires rather than as a separate person with your own dreams.

You may have sought out achievement in your life as a way of gaining attention or approval. This is another case where your parents may have treated their love and attention as a reward for good behavior rather than as your birthright. If your parents couldn't handle the full expression of your needs as a young child, you may have learned to adapt your behavior to gain their acceptance and approval. By conforming your needs to fit their limited capacities, you started to parent your parents. You consciously or unconsciously noticed and attended to their deficits, making your personality into something they could tolerate. In exchange, you may have received physical protection, conditional attention and a modicum of emotional sustenance.

By contrast, your parents may also be *threatened* by your potential achievement. They may be frightened that you are exceeding their level of accomplishment in life. They may be afraid that you are becoming autonomous and will no longer need them for your care. They may have had different ideas about your role in life, such as working in a family business, never leaving your home town or taking physical care of them. As in the previous example, your parents use your life path as a way of filling in the gaping holes in their self-confidence and shielding them from their fears of losing control or being alone.

Status-seeking and pleasing others are closely related in the sense that they are both about trying to address one's insecurities by living up to others' standards of behavior. None of this is intended to fault your parents for their impacts on you or to oversimplify their motivations. And it is not to say that you should completely ignore your parents' advice or reaction to your decision. The importance of this Naked

Truth is that it asks you to look closely at your own motivations around attending law school and make sure that they are in fact your own. Notice how you feel inside – in your mind, but also in your gut – as you consider the following questions:

- When you think about going to law school or not going to law school, how do you imagine your family will react? How much of their reaction factors into your decision-making process?

- Do you feel confident about who you are as a person and your entitlement to your own fulfillment, regardless of whether you attend law school or not?

- How was accomplishment recognized or not in your family? Did you feel fully appreciated for your successes? Did you feel seen, loved, and supported regardless of your academic, athletic or care-taking accomplishments?

THE THIRD TRUTH: LACK OF IMAGINATION

A lack of imagination is an extremely common reason for applying to law school. Talented undergraduates see their graduation approaching in the distance and they start thinking "What am I going to do with my life?" Feeling no native interests or proclivities, they see law school as an easy alternative. "Easy" here means "not requiring extended thought," not as in "easy to live with." For some reason, the smartest people you can imagine decide that they would like to stand on a conveyor belt and let life be decided for them rather than taking an active role in creating their future. Law school is a perfect fit for this line of thinking, as everything that happens between being a 1L and being a practicing attorney is scripted for you (at least, if you let it be so). If you aren't familiar with the script, here is what it looks like, particularly if you attend a top school:

YEAR ONE: Focus on getting good grades and strategically affiliating yourself with career-enhancing extra-curricular activities, such as working for legal journals. Possibly work at a law firm in your first summer.

YEAR TWO: You've gotten the hang of law school and can manage your course load. Now it's time to develop your interests and enhance your resumé with Moot Court, Law Review or other legal journals. You will participate in on-campus interviewing in the fall to line up your summer internship. This internship will potentially chart the course for your legal career. Over the summer, you get lots of exposure to the legal work you will be doing when you graduate. You will likely get paid more than you ever have before and you will be wined and dined by your firm, whose goal is to hire you when you graduate.

YEAR THREE: The idea here is to make sure nothing goes terribly wrong. If you want to, you can participate in on-campus interviews; but you will likely get an offer from the firm you interned with over the summer. If you are ambitious, you can take part in extra-curricular activities or apply to prestigious clerkships.

SUMMER AFTER GRADUATION: Attend a Bar Exam test prep course, typically funded by your future employer. Pass the bar.

FALL AFTER GRADUATION: Start working as an attorney.

That's it. It can truly be this straightforward and I know many people who have gone that path. If you go to a top school, everything is all set up for you. You are the talent and your future employers are hungry for you. Your tuition in part pays for an excellent career placement center that does all of the heavy lifting around bringing firms to campus and making sure there are plenty of jobs for everyone. At Stanford, I was blown away by how hard the Office of Career Services worked to orchestrate the busy interview season, to counsel students on their career paths and to identify options for those who decided not to become attorneys. They were hard-working and terrific people.

What could possibly be wrong with this? Isn't it ideal to enter into an endeavor where the variables are largely known and the path is clear?

There are at least two potential problems here. First, while the path is clear, it can be extremely difficult if you don't go to a top-tier[16] school. When law firms hire, they are trying to do two things: reduce their risk and buy your brand. In their minds, these are related. If you attended Harvard Law School, the odds are that you are very smart and are willing to work extremely hard. In addition, your school brand will look great as part of the firm's lawyer biographies. These bios may be listed on the law firm's web site or other marketing materials and you are simply worth more to the firm if you come with a good brand name behind you.

16 For the record, I didn't invent the concept of "top-tier." In general, you are at the top of the pecking order when it comes to hiring or clerkships if you come from a school that is considered a top five law school. Do I really mean top five? Of the 200 ABA approved schools, does only the top five matter? I think you could probably stretch it out to be the top ten; but I can assure you that your experience looking for a job or clerkship will look very different if you attend Harvard, Stanford, or Yale as opposed to Boalt or University of Michigan, for example. (Both of these are incredible law schools, by the way.)

Imagine if you were a Fortune 500 company and you wanted to hire a law firm to perform some legal work for you. If all of the attorneys from the firm came from top law schools, you might feel like it was a safe bet and that you were hiring the best. And you might actually be doing so. Even though it can feel reassuring to say that status doesn't or shouldn't matter, I think it is often reflective of quality in the legal profession. Students at the top schools excelled repeatedly and consistently in their lives in order to get into their school of choice. It doesn't mean that there are no hotshots at schools with lower rankings. But if you are a law firm making a hiring decision, you might decide that it is less risky to hire someone from a top school.[17]

If you are looking for a public interest job (i.e. a job working as an attorney for a non-profit or NGO), your path will be difficult regardless of where you go to law school. While it might seem that public interest hiring will be more humane and less competitive than looking for a job at a law firm, the opposite is often true. Public interest opportunities are much scarcer than standard for-profit law firms. There are simply fewer opportunities out there and the competition for what positions there are is intense. Further, these organizations are typically much less integrated into the on-campus interviewing process and you will need to do significantly more leg work to even get an interview. And, of course, once you start your public interest job, you will be paid significantly less than your peers who work at law firms. This is true despite the fact that your law school debt will be equally high. Some law schools have LRAP programs to assist with paying off debt, but the assistance is limited and is typically calibrated to your income.

So, while there is a path, your success is not inevitable.

But what if you do go to a top-tier law school? Or what if you aren't worried that there might be competition when it comes to finding internships, legal positions, or clerkships? If this is the case for you, I suggest that you consider whether the law path is *your* path or simply a *convenient* path. For many people, the latter is the case. If you fall in this camp, consider the following: There is a time in life to be passive or lazy about your decisions. If you buy a sweater without trying it on because you are too lazy or busy or disinterested to spend time in the dressing room, that's okay. If you don't like the sweater, you can return it, or – if you don't want to go to the trouble – you can simply accept that you are $200 poorer.

17 This analysis, however, doesn't account for regional law schools. There are many strong regional law schools that may not have a national reputation but are viewed as excellent schools in their local market. Law firms in that region may feel very comfortable hiring graduates from these schools.

Now is the time to wake up and realize that the decision to go to law school is utterly serious and should be considered with a grave and engaged mind.

This moment in your life is not the time to take the easy way out. It is not the time to have decisions made for you. Please, *please*, do not make the mistake of letting life simply happen *to* you. Law school and legal practice will swallow you up and you risk squandering your potential. Many practicing attorneys will tell you that they strongly dislike their jobs, but see no clear way out of the legal profession. They feel like the time has come and gone to experiment with career alternatives and they are trapped in a career that their hearts and minds have outgrown. Now is the time to wake up and realize that the decision to go to law school is utterly serious and should be considered with a grave and engaged mind.

I fell prey to my own lack of imagination when deciding to attend law school. Here's how I thought about the problem: I thought I had insufficient practical experience to get a good job with a career path where I could make lots of money. I saw law school as a fairly certain way to become wealthy and experience myself as smarter, more accomplished and generally more deserving of taking up space on planet Earth. Now, before you say, "Law school can give you all of those things," I should tell you that I started law school in 1998. Just as one example, eBay went public on September 24, 1998, roughly the same time I started law school. During the three years I was in law school, I lived amidst one of the fastest growing economies in the world. Millionaires were being made every day as new, innovative companies brought their stock offerings to the market. In the San Francisco Bay Area, companies were desperate to hire almost anyone and pay them handsomely.

So, when I say "lack of imagination," in my own case this would have meant opening up a newspaper and reading about the world around me. I would have found that the economy was *awash* in opportunity and going to law school at this time made absolutely no economic sense. What's interesting is that, at the time, I *did* read the newspaper. I wasn't entirely oblivious to the fact that interesting things were going on in the world of technology. I simply wasn't imaginative enough about my own capacities to think that I could get on board the gravy train myself. Though I had work experience, I somehow thought that all of the possible job roles open to me required more intelligence, experience or credentials than I had. I couldn't have been further from truth. What is fascinating to me is that, at the time, I never just sat down and thought "what else could I do besides go to law school?" I contemplated business school, but I didn't yet have enough job experience to qualify for most

...not knowing the *right* answer doesn't mean that you should accept an easy answer that you haven't considered carefully.

MBA programs. I thought I had to get a credential, like a JD or an MBA, in order to be able to get a respectable job with a promising future.

If you see in yourself a lack of imagination about your future, but need help thinking about alternatives for yourself, don't worry; we'll talk about some good starting points in a moment. But before we start thinking about alternatives, let me introduce some premises that will ground you and help you make sure you are steering your life in the right direction.

First off, not knowing the *right* answer doesn't mean that you should accept an easy answer that you haven't considered carefully. When you feel uncertain about a life decision, you may feel anxiety or pain about not knowing. Depending on your personality type, this level of uncertainty may feel unbearable and you will willingly run to any alternative that provides you a greater sense of stability. However hard it is, though, I encourage you to stick it out. Stay in your uncertainty long enough to really explore and understand the best possible direction for your life.

Second, times of uncertainty are the perfect times to start experimenting. A number of my colleagues at law school worked in law firms as paralegals or in other roles before they came to law school. That's a terrific example of experimentation, and they got paid to do it! It's fair to say that they went in to law school with a much better sense of what it would be like to work in a law firm than the rest of us. There are many other ways to experiment and we will talk about them in a moment. But the point is, if you feel stuck in indecision, try something, almost anything, and see how it feels. When you are experimenting, do so with a good head on your shoulders. Going to law school could be seen as an experiment in evaluating your interest in the legal profession. But it's an extremely expensive and time-consuming experiment that could be better executed by, for example, working at a law firm as a paralegal for a year.

Before we start talking about how to generate imaginative ideas about your future, I want to first give an example of someone for whom law school was a perfect fit. I made friends in law school with a student who lived with her boyfriend relatively near my house. We commuted from San Francisco to Palo Alto often in our first semester of law school. She was outstanding as a law student and was passionate about doing well in law school. I never had the feeling that she was unimaginative in her career choice. It was clear that she had found something that she was good at and was reveling in it. Make no mistake – she worked as hard as you can imagine – but all of her hard work made sense because law school fit so well with her personality and her aptitudes. Another interesting thing about her was that while she was motivated by her success, it was clearly for her own enjoyment and enrichment. I never experienced her as someone who sought out the approval of others at the expense of her own desires. After law school, she clerked for a Supreme Court justice (an outstanding distinction in the legal profession) and continued on to an extremely successful legal career. I mention her story here because I think it is important to emphasize that there are some people for whom legal study and practice is a beautiful fit. Legal practice is truly a magnificent expression of their abilities and interests. These people actually exist and it's possible you are one of them.

But, if you are not sure, you may be in need of some alternatives. This involves a little bit of work, but I promise you that it is worth it. First off, if you haven't seen a career counselor either as part of your university's career service or in private practice, now is the time to go. If you have already graduated, career guidance is often still made available to alumni. Career counselors are people who have typically worked with hundreds of people in very similar circumstances to you. They can help you understand your strengths, aversions and preferred work-life balance. They can translate these preferences into potential career paths that you might be interested in. It doesn't take much time (especially in comparison to the three years you will spend in law school) to get some help understanding how to make money off of work that interests you and fits with your personality. Career counselors are a great resource.

One note of caution about career counselors, especially those who are affiliated with a university: Sometimes, career counselors will not completely realize the uniqueness of your situation and personality. They might not understand that you are completely different from anyone else who has ever walked through their door. In a sense, they are suffering from a lack of imagination all their own. They might even be lazy. As a result, they might recommend career paths that make no sense to you. If this happens to you, don't be discouraged. Process the information and suggestions they provide and simply discard them as interesting, but not applicable if they do not fit your interests. Don't write off the benefits of career counseling just because you happen to have a mediocre or even bad experience with a career counselor. I promise you that a good career counselor is worth his or her weight in gold. So, keep trying.

Here is another thing you can do that is completely fun and easier than you might think: Interview working people about their own jobs and career paths.[18] This is a great way to learn first-hand about what real, working people do in their jobs and how they got there. You can typically find people to interview through your career counseling office, your alumni association or through professional groups. When you contact someone for an informational interview, remember that this is not the time to ask for a job. It's okay to tell someone you are interviewing that you are looking, but maintain the focus on them and understanding their opinions about what they do for a living. As you do this, maintain your own sense of exploration and personal discovery. Imagine yourself being the person you are interviewing and try their life on for size. Could you potentially have fun and wake up feeling good about going to work if you followed their career path?

Finally, start exercising your imagination. Spend some time by yourself or with a trusted friend imagining a variety of futures for yourself. How do you want to spend your days? Do you see yourself relaxing on a beach? Do you see yourself working every day, doing something you feel passionate about? Or do you feel more interested in family life, creativity, or spiritual growth more than any particular career path? What kind of car will you drive, if any? What kind of house will you live in? Start imagining these things and write them down. It doesn't matter if they seem impossible or don't fit together. Treat this as a stretching exercise for your imagination. Think broadly about what you can do with your life and don't be afraid to imagine for yourself exactly what you want. I believe that uncovering career alternatives to law school is this easy.

18 See also Part One and the Addendum to this guide for more information on informational interviewing. Note that talking to people about their jobs is an essential part of both the rational approach and the holistic approach to understanding the law school decision.

To recap:

- Talk to a career counselor and avail yourself of all the resources they provide to you. This may be books, personality assessments or exercises of various sorts. Use these tools to better understand your interests and possible career paths.
- Conduct informational interviews. This is fascinating and fun. Your career counselor (or even a simple search on the web) will help you plan and execute these interviews.
- Imagine various futures for yourself. As your imagination gets stimulated it will be easier for you to see interesting opportunities that may already be closer than you think.

If you do these three things and you still feel like you lack direction, persevere! Don't give up and settle for the "easy" way out by going to law school. Consider taking a job for six months or a year to test-drive certain career paths or work environments. If you are still in school, apply for internships at businesses that will give you real work and training. It's a great way to get the flavor of a particular industry or business. Above all, do whatever it takes to stay inspired.

You are creating a life for yourself and you should celebrate this moment in your life. Surround yourself with people who are on the same path or who can support you in your efforts to understand and create exactly what you want out of life. Acknowledge the fact that you are doing some of the hardest, but most interesting work you can do as a person – having the courage to discover who you are and create a life that allows you to manifest your truest capacities.

How do you know if you are choosing law school due to a lack of imagination? Consider the following questions:

- Have you explored other alternatives to law school?
- If so, how much effort have you put in to considering these alternatives? If you can only quantify this in hours or days and not weeks or months, continue your investigation.
- Have you spoken to a career counselor and conducted informational interviews?
- Have you spent time by yourself or with your friends imagining ideal futures for yourself?
- In your heart of hearts, have you felt too lazy or frightened to seriously consider your career options?

THE FOURTH TRUTH: FEAR

Fear drives many people into the arms of law school. The idea is something like this: "It's an uncertain, unstable world out there. With a law degree I'll be qualified to be an attorney, which will be a stable career path for the remainder of my days. All I need to do is go to law school and I won't have to worry about money or unemployment again. Law is a stable profession. Even in the worst of economic times, people and businesses still need attorneys. Even if it's hard being an attorney, it's much better than dealing with the vicissitudes of the marketplace, being afraid of losing your job or being deskilled because of technological changes or because your job is shipped overseas. Say what you will, law is a safe career choice."[19]

It's understandable to seek safety. The idea of creating safety for yourself far, far into the future may feel *deeply* comforting. I would go so far to say that seeking safety is a primal desire. As infants, when we are our most vulnerable, we respond to our genetic programming when we seek out the safety and comfort of our mother. This drive to connect with our mother serves our urgent needs for food, physical protection and emotional sustenance that are essential for our development, but impossible to create by ourselves. The idealized image of an infant cradled in its mother's arms is a profound expression of our primal desire for an emotional experience of complete safety and protection.

As mature adults, we use our mammalian instincts to keep an eye out for threats and to avoid danger. Our drive for safety and our fear of danger is hard-wired into our system. In our modern society, fear can be expressed in resourceful ways and in painful, divisive ways. For example, our desire for a safe environment has inspired us to create an infrastructure of traffic signals, stop signs and safe railroad crossings throughout our country. With these useful systems in place, we increase our overall safety and participate in the care of each other. Fear can be expressed in *divisive* ways when, for example, it drives discrimination or violence. People may fear change, cultural difference or a loss of control, and that can cause them to act in hurtful ways toward others. Whether fear is expressed in ways that support our best potential or not, our fear represents a fundamental aspect of our humanity. While it's wise to carefully consider your *response* to fear, the fear itself is an expression of a resourceful part of your physiology.

There is our natural aversion to fear and an instinct to seek protection; and there is law school and legal practice that hold the promise of putting an end to our worries forever. There are certainly practical considerations here. However, the idea that legal practice is a safe career choice is only half true. Its veracity lies in the fact that if you

19 I discuss these assumptions in greater detail in Part One.

choose to be an attorney for the rest of your working life, you will never have to fear making another decision about how to express your talents through your profession. Committing to legal practice fully may mean that there are certain decisions about your life that you will never have to face again.

As I mention elsewhere in this guide, this may practically be false. In every economic downturn, significant numbers of lawyers are laid off and law firms go out of business. This is consistently true and I encourage you to research this online if you have any doubts about it. In addition, the legal profession itself is structured to create uncertainty and instability. The pyramidal model wherein there are many people at the bottom (i.e. entry-level attorneys) and few at the top (i.e. partners) begs the question: Where do all of the lawyers who don't make partner go? Sometimes they are kept on as mid-level attorneys; sometimes they leave the legal profession; sometimes they move to smaller, less lucrative firms; and sometimes, if they don't take the hint, they are fired. This latter point is referred to as the "up or out" mentality, i.e. if you aren't on the partner track, there is ultimately no place for you at the firm.

Finally, there is the maturing of your own heart and mind. You may practice law for a number of years and simply decide that it's not what you want. Again, you will be forced to make a choice about your life, and it will typically be a much harder one than the choice you are facing now. As a practicing attorney, entrenched in the legal profession, it is even harder to seriously consider alternate career options. Many attorneys feel ringed in by their mortgages, their professional specialization and the fact that they have not seriously been exercising choice in their career path for many years. Ironically, experienced attorneys feel less capable of transitioning to other

It may feel like law school puts certain fears to rest for good. But, at best, it just delays fears to a point in your life where you may actually feel less capable of dealing with them.

professions than others in the business world. Because they have only focused on law for most of their adult lives, they fear they will have to start new careers at the bottom of the ladder from both a salary and a seniority perspective. This fear is sometimes so strong that it causes people to stay in the legal profession far beyond the point where they have given up on finding fulfillment in their career path. Going to a job you dislike every day is both demoralizing and frightening.

And, ultimately, that is my point about fear. It may feel like law school puts certain fears to rest for good. But, at best, it just delays fears to a point in your life where you may actually feel *less* capable of dealing with them. This is one of the undersides of the resourceful emotion of fear. If you put fear in the driver's seat, you will make decisions that are ultimately harmful to yourself. A powerful aversion to fear can permeate your decision-making process and cause you to organize your life around avoiding fear. Imagine making a choice today in the interest of avoiding fear that will have repercussions for the rest of your life. Think of yourself ten years out from now in a job that you are weary of, realizing that your fear put you in this position. What advice would you give to the *you* of today?

In addition to fear causing you to make bad decisions, it can also limit the expression of your personality. It may be hard to believe at this moment, but everyone has a way of inhabiting the world, moving in their bodies and directing their energies that is a perfect expression of their wholeness as human beings. And by "everyone", I mean "you." You have memories, feelings, and capacities inside your body and mind that can be and should be expressed fully. Imagine yourself ten years out from now having spent a decade finding, creating and following the fullest expression of who you are. Imagine how it feels when your actions in life are very closely aligned with your deepest sense of self. Even if you have had ten careers in as many years, the overall feeling that you have given your personality its fullest expression will sustain you. You will feel strong – much stronger than you can possibly imagine at this point in your life. If you lose your job or change careers, you can handle it because your dedication to yourself has built an unshakeable foundation of confidence, inner strength, and flexibility.

To better understand if fear is what's motivating you to go to law school, consider the following:

- Are you attracted to the legal profession because it seems safe and stable as a career choice?
- Would you be willing to walk away from law school if you decided that it wasn't a good fit with your personality?

- How do you handle change in your life? Have you had the experience of feeling courageous under uncertain circumstances?
- Does the prospect of legal practice express something that feels profoundly true about your personality?

THE FIFTH TRUTH: GREED

Greed may motivate you to go to law school. By "greed," I mean the motivation to acquire wealth. Many people envision legal careers as a pathway to getting rich. As mentioned earlier, this is not the case for a large majority of attorneys. Legal practice may bring you a comfortable middle-class lifestyle and it might bring you this lifestyle sooner than other careers. But, realistically, most attorneys don't make significant salaries unless they have made partner. As we have discussed already, only a tiny fraction of people who graduate from law school become partners in a law firm. Along the way to becoming partner, they pay a high price in terms of number of hours worked and life compromises. Other careers offer equal amounts of wealth with a much lower personal cost. And there is much, much more money to be made in business than there is in law.

But it's worth considering greed as a motivation. In U.S. culture, greed has a negative connotation. It typically connotes either acquisition for the sake of acquisition or the pursuit of wealth at the expense of any other consideration. Here, I'd like to consider greed somewhat differently. Think of greed not as an *excess* of desire, but rather the full expression of one's desires to the degree this can be realized through money. Through this definition, an artist would be considered greedy if they wanted all of the money required to create whatever works of art they were inspired to create. A business owner would be considered greedy if they wanted to create a business that lets them express their life's passion through their work. In this sense, I think greed is at least interesting and even positive. In general, economists concur with this assessment. Greed in economic terms is self-interest, i.e. making decisions based on capturing the greatest amount of value for yourself. This self-interest drives innovation of all kinds, contributes to significant economic growth and can be a great source of personal fulfillment.

Whether or not you see greed as healthy or dangerous, it is worthwhile to consider your relationship to money, as I guarantee you it will be on your mind while you are in law school. It is likely that the majority of students in your school will be interested in corporate law of some kind. This is primarily due to the fact that there are more jobs in this area than others. Contracts, bankruptcy, tax, patent, copyright and regulatory law are all areas that will be the focus of many in your cohort. Most of your colleagues will take on a substantial amount of debt and, for that reason alone, will be concerned about how much money they will earn after graduation. If you receive a scholarship in law school, it may be from a wealthy alumnus who made their fortune as a principal partner in a major law firm. There is no question that the world of law is a milieu where money matters.

Some people may object to the focus on material wealth. It may seem more ennobled to use your legal education in service to those who cannot avail themselves of legal services due to financial or other barriers. There are, in fact, many low-paying careers available to attorneys who are willing to defend the environment, refugees, political prisoners, juvenile offenders and civil liberties. It is fortunate that we live in a country where many law students and practicing attorneys seek out opportunities to help those who need the legal system for protection, the redress of wrongs or the safeguarding of our planet. This desire is so strong, in fact, that many law firms emphasize opportunities for *pro bono* work as a recruiting tool in attracting law students to work at their firm.

If greed, at least in part, drives you to law school, it is worth understanding and even expanding upon this as a motivation. For some, greed may be the outward expression of the other four Naked Truths. Wealth can confer status; it can be a tool to please others; it can reflect a lack of imagination about what to do with your life; and it can be a manifestation of a need to protect yourself from the uncertainties of life. Alternatively, wealth can be a material representation of your personal strengths. For example, your enrichment may be a welcome material confirmation that your career provides an outlet for your talents. In this case, your expression of your personality and your material wealth in the world are mutually reinforcing results. Finally, your wealth may be an outlet for contribution on both the personal and community level. Wealth can be a vehicle for expressing generosity and connection with the world at large. As with all things, wealth is neither all good nor all bad. It should be appreciated as a tool that can create many possible outcomes.

Some people have an ambivalent relationship to money. Privately, they will admit that they want to surround themselves with luxuries or material comforts; to the outside world, they rein in their desires, not wanting to seem overly desirous or superficial. If this is you, it is time to get out of your own way and take pleasure in wanting whatever you want. Obsessing over money, like any other obsession, can be unhealthy. But the simple act of desiring a better future for yourself, even an extraordinary future far beyond what you can currently imagine, is entirely wholesome. You might think that a focus on material wealth will exceed others' standards for decency or propriety. Whether or not this is the case, it doesn't matter. Your desire to have more is part of your personality and it should be given room to express itself fully.

We live in a wealthy society, a fact that we can be extremely grateful for and not something we have to hide from or worry about. Go ahead, play with your desire. Imagine what your life would be like and how you could express yourself in the world if there were no limits to your material success.

Consider the role of greed in your decision to go to law school:

- Is there some forum in your life – in conversation with friends or even in your imagination – where you feel completely free to express your desires fully?

- Will the money you make as an attorney satisfy your desire for wealth? What will you do if it doesn't?

- What do you want money to do for you? Are you addressing emotional needs through your desire of money? If so, take time to think about which of these feelings may need more attention.

- If you are suspicious of money or people who desire money, is your sense of identity robust enough to befriend your law school colleagues who may feel very differently? Can you imagine enlisting your upwardly-mobile colleagues as personal allies?

CHAPTER SEVEN

UNDERSTANDING YOUR POTENTIAL

An honest self-assessment of your motivations in choosing a career provides you with extremely important information about your personality. We make better decisions when we understand what makes us tick. Some people object to the idea that there is more to their personality than what lies at the surface. They have a self-concept that shuns the idea of an inner life or unconscious motivations. They see the idea of having fears or insecurities driving their actions as a personal failing, so they work hard to pretend that it's not happening. But having a multiplicity of motivations – some known and some that are not yet clear to you – is what makes us human and what keeps life interesting and dynamic.

Consider this: Have you ever had a computer, DVD player, or television that didn't quite work as expected? Maybe you periodically had to completely reboot your computer to make it work right. Or maybe you had a DVD player that was picky about which DVDs it would play. Or maybe you had a TV where one button on the remote control always got stuck. When these situations arise, there is often a period where you learn to work within the quirks of how your equipment operates. You may, overall, enjoy your computer, DVD player or TV; or maybe you are just stuck with it. So you learn to accept and work with its periodic misbehavior.

While our minds are many times more complex and interesting than a piece of electronic equipment, our *relationship* to our minds can be somewhat similar. When we honestly understand our personalities, we learn to work *with* our minds rather than *against* them. We understand our foibles, acknowledge them, and even have compassion for ourselves. But this knowledge doesn't stop us from getting the most out of life.

For example, if you have a strong desire to go to law school because you are completely afraid of not knowing what to do with your life, you can acknowledge your fear and understand that the urgency of your decision is driven by this fear and not by externally imposed deadlines. If you want to go to law school to make your parents happy, you can acknowledge your desire to please others while also turning your attention to your own strengths and self-expression. Working *with* our personalities means acknowledging ourselves as whole people – with our many strengths and frailties – and not letting our fears, doubts, insecurities or anger take over our life decisions. We acknowledge who we are at this particular moment in our lives and then make decisions informed by our *entire* personality. We put our optimism, expansiveness and greatest strengths in the driver's seat, while acknowledging the parts of ourselves that need shelter, care and continued attention.

But here's the rub: What if you acknowledge that law school may not be right for you, but you don't see any obvious alternative? You may have even performed some due diligence, such as talking to a career counselor or conducting informational interviews, but you are no closer to understanding what you want to do with your life. Self-knowledge may be useful in guiding you away from bad decisions, but can it guide you *toward* your ideal, fulfilling career?

For some, understanding what they want to do with their life has always been easy. There are many people in law school who feel this way about being a lawyer. They may have always had it in the back of their minds that they want to become attorneys. They may have been inspired all of their lives by attorneys who have broken new legal ground or expressed unique dexterity with legal argumentation. For these people, becoming an attorney has been a lifelong ambition and they don't have much internal conflict about it. These are the people for whom law school is an excellent fit.

This certainty of purpose can be found in many professions: doctors, teachers, entrepreneurs and scientists, for example, may find that the way they think about life, problem solving and self-expression perfectly clicks with their chosen profession. That is not to say that a certain amount of introspection wouldn't be beneficial; but all of the self-questioning and reflection in the world may lead them right back to the vocation they have already selected. It is their passion, their comfort and some would refer to it as their calling.

For most people, however, the waters are much murkier. I believe that those of us who don't feel an inherent professional calling are, in fact, the lucky ones. We *create* our passions and life purpose and we never stop growing as people. There is a great freedom in knowing that you are the creator of your life's purpose. It means that beyond what your family wants, beyond what society wants, even beyond your conscious motivations today, there is a future that is entirely your own, entirely of your own making. And you have an immense capacity for dealing with change. You aren't wedded to any particular profession, so you can more easily roll with the punches as the marketplace continuously expands, contracts and otherwise changes its proportions.

Most significantly, as you develop personally, your interests will change and your career can change with you. It is often said that a typical worker in the U.S. changes careers three to five times over their lifetime. As you change careers, you will find that you are exposed to new information, new personalities and new business challenges that will keep you stimulated and fulfilled. If you are afraid about not knowing what to do professionally at this moment in your life, acknowledge your fear, and take comfort in the fact that most people face the same challenge. As an evolving personality, it is unlikely that you will ultimately find a career path that is truly your final destination. Instead, you will experiment, evaluate your results, and explore your options on an ongoing basis throughout your life. As a result, you will have a chance to cultivate many parts of your personality and you will know in your bones that you never have to feel stuck where you are in life.

CHAPTER EIGHT

THE FOUR KEYS TO NO-REGRETS LIVING

There are four skills that you must cultivate as you focus on living a life of your design. Strengthening these skills will help you develop gut-level instincts that will sharpen your decision-making and increase your confidence. I call these the Four Keys to No-Regrets Living. By No-Regrets Living, I mean that these skills will guide you as you make your way through life, ensuring that every step of the way you are connecting to your truest and best intentions for yourself. "No-Regrets" doesn't mean "no mistakes." It means that your self-concept incorporates the idea of learning, trial-and-error and continued self-evaluation.

Now, brace yourself. In order to live a life without regrets, you need to take action. It is essential that you understand and *act* on the fact that this is your life to create. *Exerting your will in better understanding yourself*, even if it doesn't come naturally at first, and then *taking action in your own best interest* is the only way to make decisions that you can live with. When you make decisions based on self-knowledge, they will make sense and feel right long after the fact, even if circumstances change or you were incorrect in your assumptions. Living a life without regrets means taking action that is in alignment with an honest understanding of yourself. But it doesn't stop there. You must then constantly revisit your self-understanding and adjust your actions to account for your new discoveries about who you are today.

THE FIRST KEY: CHECKING IN

The idea of "checking in" refers to the practice of periodically evaluating where you are at in life in order to bring your focus and direction in alignment with your current and long-term needs. This task is much more difficult than it may seem. Our culture has many outlets that make it easy to live life on auto-pilot. If you feel boredom or dissatisfaction, for example, you can watch TV, surf the web, update your Facebook/MySpace/Twitter account, text your friends, etc. For some, these distractions become the star of the show, taking up much of their time when not at work (or even while at work).

Continuously feeding your mind's desire for distraction can take you very far away from who you are and how you want to realize yourself in the world.

If you work in an office, your workplace may foster distractedness. Incoming emails or phone calls combined with the imperative to multi-task means that our minds are constantly moving from one task to another, never settling in deeply on a particular activity. Continuously feeding your mind's desire for distraction can take you very far away from who you are and how you want to realize yourself in the world.

While it is wholesome to pursue outlets for your enjoyment, you cause great harm to yourself when your entertainment activities primarily function as hideouts from deeper, more complicated needs. Let me reiterate this point, because I don't want there to be any confusion: I believe that it is crucial that you have opportunities in your life – ideally every day – where you can just let go and surrender to pleasure or relaxation. These activities keep us motivated and provide some unstructured time where our minds can stumble upon unexpected inspiration. But when we feed at our computers or televisions passively, accepting what comes to us rather than making conscious choices, we risk covering up and even forgetting about what we need the most.

Imagine living a life wherein you not only fail to address your needs, you even stop realizing what your needs were in the first place. This is a true tragedy and should be avoided at all costs. There is so much good and so much fulfillment that is possible for you in your life. Letting life pass you by is a terrible waste of *you*. You have so much to offer to this world; but I wouldn't even worry about the world at this moment. You have so much to offer just to *yourself* – the opportunity to reach your life's end knowing that your personality had free reign to express itself, discover itself and fully bloom. This is one of life's most profound gifts, and it is an opportunity that you must not squander.

Checking in with yourself periodically is a way to make sure that the hungriest parts of your personality are being fed. Sometimes these aspects of your personality are difficult ones: loneliness, fear, boredom, anxiety or grief. But sometimes people neglect even the brightest parts of themselves: their desires, ambitions and creativity. All of these needs and emotions are part of you. They constitute the conscious and unconscious aspects of your psyche. They are components of your wholeness and, as such, deserve both playful and serious attention.

Practically speaking, checking in means spending time daily, weekly or monthly in dialogue with yourself. This can be done through a journaling practice. With journaling, you record your thoughts in a stream of consciousness fashion without any concern for spelling, grammar, sentence structure or readability. For many people, journaling is most effective when done by hand in a physical journal. If handwriting feels alien to you, using a computer is an option as well.

In journaling, there are no restrictions and you can really write about anything on your mind. If nothing is on your mind, feel free to write about the fact that nothing is on your mind. I suggest that you keep your journals for the rest of your life, or as long as it feels right. I have been journaling for many years and I cannot fully express the sense of confidence and joy that I feel knowing that I carry my inner dialogues in material form and can refer back to them years later.

If you have a daily or weekly journaling practice, I believe that no additional structure is required. If you only journal less frequently, such as once a month, some structure is useful. For a monthly journal entry, be sure to consider the following points:

First, spend a few minutes in free-form writing. Perhaps write about your physical location, what you have done during the day, or whatever is on your mind.

> *Example*: I'm sitting in bed at home on Saturday morning. I just woke at 11:00 and I'm still waking up…

Second, take some time to consider what you have needed this month. Give an emotional snapshot of what life has been like either through free-form writing or in a bullet list.

> *Example*: I've had a great time this month hanging out with friends and I find myself always wanting to check in with people to see what's going on…I was really frustrated with the feedback I got on my History paper…I'm getting bored with basketball…

Third, consider your activities for the month. What have you been doing to attend to your needs?

> *Example*: Spending time with friends has been great for me. I've really felt the pleasure of being with people and having fun…I thought about talking to my History professor about the paper, but I was so pissed off I didn't even bother…Basketball satisfies my desire to move around and play a game that I like. But something is missing for me…

Finally, spend some time imagining your future. What are you looking forward to right now in your life? What rewards would you enjoy, even if they seem currently unattainable? What are you doing right now that is helping you address your needs and goals?

> *Example*: I really want to plan a trip with my friends during the next holiday break…I also would love to have a really great date with someone interesting that I haven't met yet…I love going to concerts and I see myself being able to see any show I want, regardless of how much it costs.

In the once-a-month approach, I suggest spending an hour considering these questions or take them one-by-one over the course of a weekend. The goal is not to spend a specific amount of time; rather, spend *sufficient* time to really take stock of where things are at in life for you. Again, the goal is to understand what life has been like for you, what you have done to attend to your needs, what needs have gone unmet and what kind of future you imagine for yourself.

If journaling just isn't your thing, there are many other ways to check in with yourself. You can have a regular conversation with someone you trust; you can take walks with your friends where you discuss and imagine your futures; you can spend time just letting your mind wander over the topics described above.

As you consider your life, don't feel pressured to make your interests seem productive or wholesome. On the days when you are filled with ambition, you will have ambitious thoughts. On days that you are filled with hedonism, you will have hedonic thoughts. Accept yourself for where you are at and trust that the act of checking in with yourself is enough to ensure that your internal guidance system is driving you in the right direction.

There is no right or wrong way to check in with yourself. The key is to incorporate into your personality and your habits the idea that you are a person with specific needs and desires and you align your life activities to address these desires. If I were to say what is truly at the heart of checking in, it is this very idea: *alignment.* In order to experience alignment in your life, two things must be true: You must have an idea about what you want and you must consistently act in a way that brings about the outcomes that you desire. Checking in guides you toward living a life in alignment by making sure that you take the pulse of how your needs are evolving and adjust your actions accordingly.

THE SECOND KEY: EXPERIMENTATION

Now, you may have just read all of this and thought "it would be so much easier to just suck it up and go to law school rather than deal with a long-term process of cultivating self-knowledge." I know. It isn't easy and it doesn't necessarily feel concrete. Getting to know yourself and your experience deeply is challenging, in part due to the adaptability of our minds. We often experience the world in terms of activities we are averse to and those we desire. We move away from our aversions and move toward our desires. Much has been said on this topic elsewhere, but I bring it up to mention that sometimes our deepest hurts, disappointments or traumas are so profound that they powerfully motivate us toward activities that keep us from having to re-experience the same pain. This is true even when the danger we once faced is no longer present. Turning *toward* the most sensitive parts of your personality is going against the grain of what feels safe for your mind.

But the Second Key, Experimentation, makes it all easier. The fact is that you don't *have* to know all of the answers in order to live a life that is profoundly fun and fulfilling. This is particularly relevant when considering career alternatives. As I have mentioned earlier, when considering a direction for your career, talking to career counselors and conducting informational interviews is a great way to do research. But this doesn't guarantee that you will come up with an answer as to the perfect next step in your career. This is the point that makes many people nervous – what if you just don't know yet how to get from here to a $100,000 annual salary?

The trick is to just try *something.* As long as it's not actively harmful to you, getting started in almost any career will provide you with great information about your likes and dislikes and it will expose you to people who will become your champions as your career progresses. This might sound good in theory, but I want to make it as concrete as possible. Using all of the tools at your disposal – your alumni network, friends, contacts you've made in informational interviews, on-campus interviewing, Craigslist, etc. – start looking for jobs in career areas that provide at least *some* interest for you. Go to job interviews, even if you aren't 100% sure you are interested in the job being offered.

Remember, you're not looking for the "ultimate" job; you are looking for a fertile environment where you can learn, get real-world experience, meet people and discover your likes and dislikes. When you are evaluating potential jobs, consider the following:

> Will this position provide opportunities for me to learn about a new subject matter or get practical experience in an area that may be of value to me in the future?
>
> Will the people I'm working with be interesting or fun? Can I see them championing me as I move forward in my career?
>
> Will the activities I'm doing be at least tolerable or, if not, is there opportunity for growth in the future?

This may be a different mindset than you are used to. Instead of groveling in front of potential employers, you are subjecting them to a scrutiny of your own. It's important not to come across as arrogant in the interview process – let your future employer know that you are interested in the company and eager to contribute. But inside, know that even a terrific-sounding job offer is something to consider in light of your overall goals.

Here's a secret: if you are currently considering going to law school, it is very likely that you are already a leader amongst your peers. By that, I mean you may excel academically, you may be uniquely ambitious or you might have a good knack for picking things up in whatever environment you find yourself. When you work in your first experimental job, it is very likely that you will easily and, possibly, accidentally *shine*. If you keep your eyes open and act with faith and purpose[20], you will attract positive attention and see new opportunities open for you. How am I so sure of this? I've seen it happen again and again. The business world is hungry for people who are smart, creative, competent and flexible. If you can get your foot in the door, you will

20 I borrow the idea of faith and purpose from Wallace Wattles.

be recognized and appreciated. This is particularly true in a business that is growth-oriented and has other clever people as employees.

If this all sounds good, but also seems like I'm describing someone who isn't at all you, I offer you this: Your self-assessment of your capacities is limited if you lack real-world experience. If you are about to graduate from undergraduate or graduate school, you have been taught that excellence is about studying subjects, developing mastery and then taking a test. The work world tends to work in the exact opposite order. Every day is a new test and your experience over time is what truly brings mastery. If you don't feel confident in your abilities now, just jump in and do your best. Good intentions and diligent effort will be appreciated by your employer.

What if absolutely nothing sounds interesting? You've read up on marketing, sales, accounting, teaching, being a tour guide and performing on Broadway and nothing really strikes a chord with you? This is great news! Why? It means that you have complete flexibility to experiment with *anything*. No career path could truly be a bad idea if none of them seem good. You have no chance of missing out on a great opportunity if all opportunities are equal.

One final note about generalized disinterest: As a being in this world, it is your responsibility and your opportunity to create your own joy. It may come as a surprise, but creating your happiness actually requires *effort*. As infants, our happiness is provided to us in the form of love, attention and a stomach full of warm milk. As we grow older, we learn to create our own happiness by seeking out new sources of joy and meaning. These sources of meaning could be our interactions with friends, creative activities, making money, volunteering and almost anything else. If this sounds alien to you, cultivating a spirit of experimentation and effort are good first steps to bringing new opportunities to your life.

THE THIRD KEY: FLEXIBILITY

Closely related to the idea of Experimentation is Flexibility. In general, flexibility means being able to adapt to circumstances that are counter to your desires or expectations. It can also mean that you monitor your circumstances and adjust your direction as you gather new information. Having a sense of flexibility is essential to being able to experiment in the first place. For example, you may find yourself with a job offer for a position that isn't in your ideal field or function. Alternatively, you may find yourself with absolutely no job offers at all. With a flexible attitude, you can enter into situations even if they aren't exactly as you imagined. You can take in data (such as, "there are no entry-level jobs in my desired field right now") and adjust your strategy. Being flexible means that you accept what is before you today with the understanding that you are moving toward an increasingly brighter future.

In addition to helping you find a job in the first place, being flexible is an essential workplace skill. In the work world, things seldom go exactly as planned. Improvisation, working with limited resources (i.e. not enough people or money) and thinking on-the-fly are the norm. If you can maintain a flexible attitude under imperfect circumstances, you will quickly win the respect and admiration of your peers. In this sense, flexibility is an emotional skill that will make you money and help you build a career.

There are certain circumstances where *in*flexibility is important – setting personal boundaries, refusing to participate in inhumane or unjust activities or simply standing up for yourself when the time is right. Being flexible doesn't mean turning off your critical faculties in the face of bullying or abuse. In fact, finding some inflexibility will feel empowering for people who were taught to submit to others' needs in the interest of respecting authority or acting with humility. Asserting your desires strongly and perhaps inflexibly may present an opening for you, a chance to stretch your personality and find a new, more resourceful voice inside yourself.

But, often, inflexibility has less to do with taking a stand than with asserting control.[21] The dark side of control comes out when we need to constrain our self-concept or control others in order to avoid our deepest fears, disappointments, and resentments. For example, if you have parents who are in professional careers – i.e. doctors, lawyers, professors, etc. – you may feel like you need to pursue a career with an equal level of social status. You may reject other careers simply because they don't afford the same level of status, not because those career paths aren't right for you. By maintaining an inflexible self-concept, you limit your ability to experience your life in its fullest. You hide from the idea that you are worthy of attention and respect regardless of your career path. And you cower from the possibility of not meeting your parents' expectations.

Another way in which inflexibility and asserting control undermine our thinking is when we stick to bad decisions, even when the data tells us we should change course. For example, you may have taken the LSAT and sent in your law school applications. You might have even been accepted to several law schools. But you have a sinking feeling inside of you that law school truly isn't the right path. Changing your mind may make you fear that others will perceive you as weak. You may even

21 Asserting control is not always a bad thing. The world is unpredictable and we all need to feel some level of control over our lives. Feeling "in control" means that we don't have to constantly be on the lookout for threats in our environment. It also allows us to feel confident in our capacities.

be trying to maintain your self-image just to yourself – you are the kind of person who doesn't quit, who is decisive, who finishes things. In the face of this kind of inflexibility, you might ask yourself what you are trying to prove and to whom. Why does taking in new information and acting in accordance with that new information seem like a sign of weakness or failure inside of you? Try replacing this inflexible belief with the idea that intelligent people monitor their circumstances and make new decisions based on the data they collect. Not only is this a smart way to think about life decisions, changing your mind is something you are entitled to do as a thinking being.

When you are not limited to a predetermined set of options and your self-concept is robust, you will see more possibility to make a living in interesting and lucrative ways.

Flexibility is essential when exploring new career paths. Experimentation requires that you try new things. Flexibility gives you the power to persevere in circumstances that aren't exactly what you expected and then change course when you have collected sufficient information to indicate that a change is necessary. Flexibility necessarily generates more opportunity for you in your career. When you are not limited to a predetermined set of options and your self-concept is robust, you will see more possibility to make a living in interesting and lucrative ways. With a flexible perspective, you have the confidence to know that you can handle life's vicissitudes while keeping an eye out for new opportunities.

An adjunct skill to flexibility is what I call "keeping your eyes open." With a flexible outlook, you have the ability to imagine positive outcomes, even in the face of difficult or uncertain circumstances. Take this moment in your life right now as an example. If you are among those who are considering law school because you don't know what else to do with your life, some flexibility and keeping your eyes open is in order. Right now, you may see the certainty of law school on the one hand and the uncertainty and fear of an unknown alternative on the other. Even if law school itself isn't appealing, certainty may feel safer to you than uncertainty. But here is what I promise will happen to you if you act with flexibility – you will start to see opportunities around you that you had never seen before. Even if you don't see them now, they are there and they are waiting for you. When you start experimenting in your life and adopt a flexible attitude, the world changes because something inside *you* starts to change. Opportunities for making money, doing something you love or having an impact with your life become more apparent to you because you are willing to take chances and be flexible about the outcomes.

THE FOURTH KEY: LIFE ON YOUR OWN TERMS

I have a deep conviction that your direction in life should be determined by your deepest needs and capacities, not the desires, expectations or beliefs of others. This may seem provocative to some, especially if you have been taught that putting others first is the best way to express compassion and humility. You may be afraid that living life on your own terms is at odds with the way you express charity or kindness; you may feel that the pain of disappointing others is greater than the pain of suppressing your own needs; or, you may have had experiences of being bullied by others' selfish and controlling demands. All of this makes you think that living life on your own terms is too prideful, too selfish and too open for abuse.

There are several reasons why I believe that these fears are misplaced. First and foremost, there is simply no way to leverage your resourcefulness in helping others (if that is where you wish to direct your energies) if you have relegated your own needs to second-class citizens. A failure to acknowledge and attend to your own needs has many negative consequences:

> While your passion for others may start off strong, your single-minded focus will ultimately result in resentment or depression. You will have no energy to help others, because you have neglected the parts of your personality that are the engines of your own vitality.
>
> Your compassionate stance may become a thinly veiled form of control or contempt.
>
> You may become dependent on the gratitude of others to support your ego.
>
> Your anger about the world's injustices may turn painful when it is really misdirected rage about your own lack of emotional nourishment.

If you are on a chronic diet of self-sacrifice, you will become much less clear about your actions and decisions; you will be less equipped to make smart choices and find creative solutions; and you will be motivated – even if only unconsciously – by your pain rather than your best thinking. Worst of all, you will be ceding parts of your personality that deserve expression. Unexpressed aspects of your character will atrophy and may be forgotten entirely.

Second, it is a misjudgment of others' resilience and personal responsibility to assume that they cannot handle the full expression of who you are. If it is painful for you to imagine disappointing others, it is worth considering the nature of this pain and the true weight of disappointment. Life is filled with disappointments. While we may appreciate life's gifts overall, it doesn't mean that every day doesn't have its fill of thwarted desires and expectations that aren't met. No one can truly be shielded from life's disappointments. Life, in fact, *requires* a certain amount of resilience from us. If you became immobilized every time your favorite team lost a game, you couldn't find a parking spot or it rained during spring break, it would be difficult to function in life. Our resilience allows us to express our disappointment and anger and keep moving forward with our lives. We may have dashed hopes, but we don't stop dreaming.

If disappointing others is frightening or painful for you, you may be underestimating the ability of others to manage their own feelings. Or, if you are certain about others' reactions, you may be forgetting that – as an adult – it is not your responsibility to preserve others' peace of mind at your own expense. If you are willing to make bad decisions for yourself in order to avoid disappointing other people, you should consider why this fear is so strong.

Many people have a deep-seated anxiety that they cannot be accepted in the fullness of their self-expression. As infants, we seek unconditional love and attention. We nourish our psyches – and, as a consequence, develop confidence and self-esteem – by having this period in our lives where we can relax into our moment-by-moment experience without the fear of rejection from our parents. If you have never had that experience, if a sense of self-confidence hasn't made its way into the marrow of your being, you might live in fear that if you truly express yourself, you will be abandoned.

Finally, I believe that it is worthwhile to make a distinction between selfishness and exploitation. When we are selfish, we realistically take into account our own needs when making decisions about our lives. We do this as a way of thinking clearly and honestly about who we are, what we are ready for and what we have to give. Our decisions may disappoint others – sometimes deeply. But we have confidence in the resilience of others and in the necessity of living an authentic life for ourselves.

Being exploitive, on the other hand, is about *controlling* others and turning our backs on our deepest needs. At the extreme end, physical abuse is exploitive of others in that it uses other people as a way of channeling our anger or fear. Rather than learning to understand and face their feelings, the exploitive person channels their feelings into abusive behavior. A less extreme example is the person who repeatedly flakes on commitments rather than revealing their ambivalence about the commitment when it is initially made. Through this lens, selfishness is about having healthy self-esteem and self-understanding; exploitation is about adopting harmful behaviors in the interest of avoiding one's fears. It is completely possible to live life on your own terms without being exploitive.

Living life on your own terms in your career is a combination of everything we have discussed so far:

- Understand yourself through journaling or other forms of reflection.
- Gather information from others through career counseling or informational interviews.
- Experiment with your career choices. Try options that may seem imperfect, as long as they are not harmful.
- Maintain a sense of flexibility and hopefulness. Monitor your surroundings for new opportunities and information. Be thoughtful about your choices and change course when the time is right.

Through this imperfect roadmap, you will find your way to a full expression of your life's potential.

When you start experimenting in your life and adopt a flexible attitude, the world changes because something inside you starts to change.

CHAPTER NINE

YOUR VOICE FROM THE FUTURE

When we embark on new ventures in life, we lack – due to the very novelty of the experience – all the knowledge that we need to avoid the pitfalls that are in front of us. Sometimes, we are in the midst of making the biggest mistakes – disasters playing out like a slow-motion car crash – without realizing the trouble we've gotten ourselves into. After we've fallen, in the midst of picking ourselves up off the ground, we lament that we weren't better prepared, that we didn't see the stumbling blocks that are now, and often painfully, obvious to us.

To a degree, there is no way around this problem. As long as we are trying new things, we will stumble, fall and pick ourselves up over and over again. This process of stumbling and recovery shapes our personality and defines our resilience. Our personalities evolve in life more through our challenges and failures than through coasting by on easy wins. As we tumble towards the ground, if we stay curious about our descent and the pain that sometimes follows, we actually become smarter, stronger, bolder and, well, more interesting as people.

While it may be impossible, and even undesirable, to avoid new experiences and new mistakes in life, wouldn't it be nice if a voice of wisdom could guide you on your journey? What if you could take your best thinking from your future and send it back in time to kindly and caringly guide you? What if a voice from your future could be on the lookout for you, trying to guide you around (or through) the toughest passes on your trek?

> **Experiment with your life not in the interest of eradicating the uncertain parts of yourself, but to the end of better understanding who you are.**

The goal of this book has been to provide that "wise voice from the future." I've made plenty of interesting decisions on my own path and I've learned a lot along the way. My own experiences have shown me that while you can't always make perfect decisions, having a framework for decision-making is a powerful tool and one that is lacking in most people's life skills repertoire. But I'll be honest with you: it's been a few years since I was in law school. Times change and memories transform from a photo-realistic picture (rich with skinned knees and bloody noses), to a soft-focused postcard from an increasingly distant yesterday.

It's for this reason that I want to provide you with up-to-the-minute data and opinions about what's happening *right now* for law school students. To this end, I have surveyed and personally spoken with law students who are in the midst of their law school labors. These students – mostly 2L's – have shared with me their personal opinions, stories and "I wish I had it all to do over again" regrets. I encourage you to treat their stories as voices from your own future. Imagine that you applied to law school, started classes a year ago and had time to sit down and reflect on your experience. While the stories I'm about to share with you come from other people's lives, try to inhabit these experiences, imagine these voices are your own voice looking back through time, providing you with the wisdom of hard-earned lessons learned.

Of course, while I think this information will be most useful to you if you really imagine it as your own voice from the future, I should add one warning here: While I believe that these perspectives are indeed very representative of a typical cross-section of law school students, none of these students have the exact same background, personality and skills that you do. If someone says something that feels like it pulls the rug out from underneath you, that's ok. Just take a deep breath, find out what information is useful in their comments and keep reading. I would say the same thing if you read something that leaves you excited and enthusiastic. Note that something inside you has been sparked, but keep reading to make sure that you are taking in all the information here, not just the parts that feel good.

First, let me provide you some background on the law students to whom I spoke. The students are from a respected, local law school. We're not talking Stanford, Harvard or Yale here; rather, a law school that more reflects the backgrounds and interests of a typical cross-section of law students. Given that, I actually don't think the responses would have varied significantly if they had been from students attending a top-five law school. Across the board, the interests and concerns of students tend to be similar: excitement about the experience of being a law student, anxieties about debt and jobs and a struggle with the significant amount of work required just to keep up.

I asked students about a variety of topics, including what led them to law school, the details of their applications, what surprised them about law school and their advice to future students. My data comes from both surveys and one-on-one, in-depth conversations. In order to get the best, sometimes brutally honest, information I promised respondents anonymity both for themselves and their school. To respect those wishes, I have slightly changed some responses while keeping the overall message intact.

WHY LAW SCHOOL?

My first interest in speaking to students was to find out what led them to law school. Was law school always in the cards? Or was it a choice arrived at later in life? Forty percent of students reported that they always wanted to go to law school, while sixty percent became curious about law school during or after college. Roughly a quarter of respondents started thinking about law school less than two years before graduation. A small, but provocative, percentage started thinking about law school as long as eight years after graduating from their undergrad.

The motivations for applying to law school were exciting, as they very much fit with the theme of this book: decisions that both make sense and feel right. Sixty-three percent of respondents said they applied to law school because it fit with their interests; forty-eight percent said they applied to law school because it fit with their personality; and forty percent said that it was the next logical career move. (Note that respondents could choose more than one answer.) Without question, these answers reflect the fact that law school is an easy and even obvious fit for many students.

Interestingly, the next highest answers are that students applied to law school in the hope of making money (37%) and because they didn't know what else to do (33%). I flag this as compelling because these are both motivations we have already discussed. These real-world responses validate that the Five Naked Truths discussed earlier in this book are as relevant as ever.

In her own words, one highly-motivated student described her decision to apply to law school with confidence:

> *"Growing up, I'd always been told I had the personality to be a lawyer. I had a go-getter attitude and did not take 'no' for an answer. I graduated with a BA in Psychology in a depressed economy. I got a job as a receptionist at a nationwide law firm and was not challenged by the work I performed in that position. I'm looking forward to graduating and having this degree that no one can ever take from me. I will never have to worry about someone else supporting me because I know I can use this degree to get a good job that will pay the bills."*

In some ways, this respondent has a classic law student profile: motivated, ambitious, proud and self-sufficient.

Several other students were attracted to law school by the real-world impacts of its practice:

> *"After discovering academia was a lot of arguing, but not necessarily a lot of changing the world, I wanted a job that would not only provide me with security but would give me the tools to improve my society. Law school seemed like a good way to combine those interests."*

Another student wrote, in a similar vein:

> *"I've always been passionate about working towards the public interest and greater social justice. Law school is a great way to gain the skills and tools that will help further those interests. In addition, I'm very competitive and thought I might enjoy the adversarial nature of the legal profession."*

And, finally, criminal law was compelling to many students who saw the practice as a profoundly tangible expression of their academic training. I quote from three different students here:

> *"I've always been interested in criminal prosecution. I made a point to work at as many District Attorney offices as possible to make sure that is what I wanted to do. The people and experiences at those offices affirmed what I believed I wanted to do."*

"I was working in criminal defense as a paralegal and I fell in love with the work. I applied to law school knowing that I wanted to become a public defender."

"The legal field has always been an interest of mine, and with my Criminal Justice undergraduate degree, I felt it was the absolute next step."

What I enjoy about all of these responses is that they reflect a high level of clarity about what brought these students to law school in the first place. As voices from one of your possible futures, I hope they challenge you to be able to articulate for yourself why law school makes sense (or doesn't) for you.

CHALLENGES AND REGRETS

Looking back, many students are happy about their decision to go to law school; yet, many wish they had followed a different path. I provide these responses without commentary, as they stand strongly on their own. As you read these, reflect on your own motivations for considering law school. Is there a possible future for you in which you would express these regrets?

"I don't regret attending law school in the least, but many of my peers wish they had never even considered it. A good friend of mine applied to law school in order to get a job at a firm. She wanted to earn a lot of money, drive expensive cars, etc. She had a trust fund set up for her grad school education, but when the recession hit she wound up taking out a loan. Now, she can't find a job at a firm because she's not a straight-A student and does not go to a top-10 school. Jobs have been slashed, she's saddled with debt, and she doesn't really have a contingency plan. She never considered what type of law she would actual enjoy practicing because she was so focused on becoming a financial success. As far as I know, her perspective on law school is the rule rather than the exception for others like her at similar schools."

"I definitely made the right choice. Law school fits perfectly with my personality. However, I also know people who regret their decision. Generally, they fall into three camps. In the first group are those that don't enjoy the adversarial and competitive nature of law school and the legal profession. They may have been better suited to going into a different graduate program, particularly social work. In the second group are those that are so competitive, they have difficulty coping with the fact that they aren't the smartest or most talented student in the room. The final group are those that went to law school because they didn't know what else to do. They might have been more satisfied with their decision if they had taken time off between undergrad and law school and/or spent more time analyzing what they really want to do."

"I do not regret it and am very happy with my decision. There are, however, a lot of people who regret it. You have to be prepared to start law school, put your head down, and work. People who came in without a clear idea of why they were going to law school or what exactly it entailed seem to be the ones struggling the most."

Some students provided honest and poignant descriptions of their current struggles:

"Career prospects suck. Classmates are worse. Just feel like I am trying so hard for something that may not even pan out. Depressed about the financial situation. Kind of wish I would have gone to med school instead (I was a bio major and had the grades to get into medical school--just didn't know if it was right for me). Now I am thinking medical school was the answer, not law school."

"The competitiveness is a major turnoff for me. You always feel like you need to be doing something more because you know that everyone else is. You feel guilty when you aren't working. People aren't blatant about their competitiveness but are very sly about always working in private. They say things like 'I haven't been keeping up on my work or reading and have so much to do' then they receive the top grades in the class. They can succeed in lulling you into a false sense of security that not everyone is working hard."

"Too expensive, not enough job security."

"Not as good as job security as expected."

"I wish I hadn't come so soon after college."

"I have a friend who regrets attending law school. He came straight from undergrad without taking any time off, and only attended because it seemed like a safe way to get employment. He hates it and wishes he had pursued a career in advertising."

Finally, many students were happy about their law school decision:

"I am lucky and love my school. I think that it is because of the group of friends that I found and the amazing city we are in."

"I do not have any regrets. However, I consider myself lucky because I have really enjoyed school and feel like I belong here, despite that I honestly did not know what to expect. I think potential law students who have more experience with the legal field (I'm specifically thinking if family members attended law school or are currently practicing) are at an advantage in making their decision and it being the right decision."

ADVICE FROM THE FUTURE

I asked law students to turn their attention to you, right at this moment in time where you are considering whether or not law school is right for you. They jumped at the opportunity, with a host of hard-hitting advice. Again, I present their comments in their original form and I leave it to you to draw your own conclusions:

> *"My advice would be that any potential law student should know that they want to do law. If you go into school thinking that you might fall in love with it, you won't have the motivation to actually complete the work, unless you really want to get it down."*

> *"Potential students should ask themselves if they really see themselves doing law for the rest of their life. They should also decide whether or not they're willing to commit to a program that will place a person in an oversaturated job market with less job security than most students believe.*
>
> *Although law school is different for everyone, it IS as hard as everyone says it is. It is never 'not that bad' or 'not as bad as people say.' Be prepared to work hard."*

> *"Don't go to law school straight from college. Don't go to law school—or any grad school—just because you are unsure of what else to do. There is a reason why attorneys are known for being miserable and dissatisfied in life, and feel as though they are caught in the rat race.*
>
> *Go to law school if you are passionate about the law. If you are unsure whether you want to be an attorney, get a job as a paralegal or volunteer somewhere for a year or so. Or talk to lawyers, or professors or law students. If you want to litigate (i.e. you love to debate), go sit in court.*
>
> *Remember, law school is an investment. There is no sense in earning your J.D. if you aren't going to capitalize on the opportunities you will have after you graduate, either in terms of realizing your increased earning potential or in terms of feeling fulfilled in your career."*

> *"1. Take at least a year off before you make a decision. Take this time to figure out what you're interested in and how a law degree would help you in that area of interest.*
>
> *2. Don't go if you don't get into a decent school. The loans are predatory and everyone is not guaranteed a good job.*
>
> *3. Don't expect an experience like undergrad. You're going to be working a lot harder. The people who don't succeed are the people who want law school to be like undergrad. Be ready for something more challenging and more work intensive, and that requires a good deal more maturity."*

"What advice?
I would recommend sitting in on a couple of classes in law school in different subjects. This would allow you to see the atmosphere of the class and understand the vibe.
What questions?
Ask yourself if you are prepared to deal with the huge load of reading you have to do nightly.
Ask yourself if you can devote the next 3 years of your life to this JD degree.
Ask yourself if you are really motivated to take on something of this magnitude.
Potential students should know...
That it's not as cut-throat as some people make it out to be.
You make a lot of great friends in law school.
The challenge of law school is really quite rewarding."

"Potential students should understand that it is not an extension of undergrad, but a major life decision that will change the way they think and perhaps even their personality. It's more work than you can imagine, and requires self-motivation. They should not attend because they cannot come up with anything else to do with their time."

"Law school is a huge investment of your time, money, and energy. It's also a very tough job market for many legal specialties. If you are going into it just because of the money or that you have heard it is an all-purpose degree, you may want to reconsider. Be honest about your personality and your interests. There is definitely room for a broad spectrum of individuals, but keep in mind that law school tends to be dominated by certain competitive personalities. Before you take the plunge, try to shadow a practicing attorney and current law student. See if their day-to-day activities are something you could see yourself doing. Once you are in law school, try to keep some perspective and balance. The reading can be long and dry, but it is all worth it when you realize how much hard work it takes to become a competent and successful lawyer. Try to find friends and activities that aren't associated with law school."

"The biggest piece of advice I can give an incoming law student is to come into law school with your head on straight. If you are upset or distracted it is going to negatively affect your ability to concentrate at the time when you need to be more prepared and focused.
Go to law school for yourself. Don't go because your parents think it's a good idea or because you'll make a lot of money. Go to law school because it's what YOU want to do. You're the one who has to put in the effort and time and you're the one who will fail or succeed."

"I think law school is a horrible waste of money unless you are pretty sure you want to do it. So, don't waste your time and money if you're just looking for something to do while

you figure out your life. Law school is not for everyone. On the other hand, there are many things one can do with a law degree that are not necessarily law related. In that regard, a law degree is one of the most helpful degrees one can have."

"Law school is really difficult and requires one to be mature and stay on top of the ball. But, it is extremely rewarding and intellectually stimulating. The people in law school are not as competitive as you think, but everything does revolve around grades. If you're thinking about law school, it does help to take classes on government in college."

"Law school is hard work and, unfortunately, it is hard to find out whether you'll like it before you get into it. My biggest suggestion is to take a law-type class in college, especially from a JD. I took business law in college, liked it, and realized after starting law school the professor had run it pretty similarly to actual law classes.
I'd also suggest you ask yourself whether you'd still be happy even if you're not the best in law school. School isn't determinative of your entire future, but it can be a frustrating three years if you're used to being the best and find yourself working really hard and struggling to understand and possibly encountering classmates who have a head for the law and may have a lot more success. Basically, you have to be willing to see all of the effort and struggle as an investment in the future. Otherwise, law school can be really disheartening."

I'll be the first to admit it: this chorus of voices, calling to you from your future, doesn't exactly sound happy. It would be easy to read the above and become discouraged. So many of these students prophesize doom and hardship rather than fun and excitement. Why is this?

I actually don't think it's because these students are trying to scare you away from law school. I think it's actually the opposite. When you have been living and breathing the law for a year or two, you become passionate about what you've been through and passionate about where you are headed. This chorus of voices isn't singing a song of doom, they are singly loudly and passionately so that all of your fear, confusion, ambition and desire come into sharp relief. As I spoke with many of these students, I had the feeling that they were earnestly and passionately speaking to you from a place of encouragement, caring and concern. The message I heard loud and clear was that law school is a challenge that should be undertaken by those who understand the challenge and who are passionate about the law.

THE CHOICE

If you've made it this far, you have all the information you need to make the right choice for yourself as to whether or not you should go to law school. If you have completed all of the exercises in this book, you have assessed both rational factors and personality factors. You have looked at the return on investment for law school; you have identified attributes and success criteria for your career path, and evaluated law and other careers in light of this; you have taken an honest look at your motivations for going to law school; and you have taken the first steps needed to better understand your life's potential. I fervently hope that whatever decision you have made, it is one that affirms your life and makes sense at a deep level.

If you are still uncertain about whether or not you want to go to law school, allow me to leave you with some thoughts on fear and uncertainty. This time, I'm not talking about fear of social censure, fear for your safety or fear of failure. I'm talking about a surprising and insidious form of fear that affects more people than you might imagine: fear of your potential and your greatness. It is an unexpected circumstance that anyone could be afraid of more success, more happiness and more full expression of their personalities. Yet, every day, this condition undermines people's aspirations, self-confidence and vitality.

Why are people afraid of their own potential? Sometimes, people avoid their potential in service to a world view they have never paused to question. They conform to the social and professional standards around them, rather than imagining their lives on their own terms. Other times, people fear their potential in service to the people around them. Their parents or peers may hold them in a certain light and stepping outside that light feels like stepping into an uncertain darkness.

Realizing your full potential in life means rising to the level of your own greatness. You may not know what that looks like right now. You might not fully understand how to create a life that expresses *you* perfectly. For the moment, you can accept your uncertainty as part of your personal development. Honor your uncertainty like it is something precious. Experiment with your life not in the interest of eradicating the uncertain parts of yourself, but to the end of better understanding who you are. If you live with your uncertainty, treat it as a companion who is along for the ride at this point in your life. You are honoring the fullness of who you are. This, in and of itself, is an act of veneration that will foster calm and self-acceptance inside of you. As you continue to experiment and refine your understanding of what is possible in your life, you will build a sense of possibility for yourself that is far beyond anything you currently know. Your uncertainty may be an indicator that now is not the right time to choose. It is the time to investigate, practice and dream.

ADDENDUM

TIPS ON INFORMATIONAL INTERVIEWING

I have woven the idea of informational interviewing throughout this book. If you are the kind of person who hates talking to strangers, it may feel like a big stretch to set up meetings with people you don't know. Well, it's time to do some stretching. There is almost no better resource for career information than people who actually have careers. It may come as a surprise, but people are generally interested in helping you and don't see an informational interview as a big inconvenience.

To reiterate, anyone considering law school or any new career needs to conduct several informational interviews. If you apply to law school without ever talking to a lawyer about their job, you are profoundly short-changing yourself.

There are many web sites that discuss informational interviewing. I encourage you to explore them. Here are some tips that will help get you started.

PRACTICE INFORMATIONAL INTERVIEWING. It might seem strange, but you will gain some confidence if you can practice the informational interview with a friend. Be sure to practice the entire process, from scheduling the interview to conducting the interview itself.

SIMPLIFY THE SOCIAL INTERACTION. If you are uncomfortable asking for help, don't make an informational interview be a meeting over lunch or dinner. Instead, suggest a ten- to fifteen-minute phone conversation. That can be plenty of time to ask the questions you need.

IMAGINE THAT YOU ARE SOMEONE ELSE. Peculiar advice, I know. If it helps, though, pretend you are a newspaper reporter or a police investigator. Your goal is to uncover interesting information that your interviewee has.

While it is important to be polite and appreciative, remember that your goal is not to make friends with your interviewee, it is to gain the information that they have generously offered to share with you.

WRITE DOWN YOUR QUESTIONS. Make sure that your interviews accomplish the goal that you have set out. The best way to do this is to write down all the points you want to cover before you start the conversation. Take notes on the responses that your interviewees provide.

ALWAYS, ALWAYS, ALWAYS STICK TO YOUR COMMITMENT. If you have told your interviewee that you want to speak with them at 10:00 a.m. on Wednesday, it is unacceptable to forget to call them. It is okay to cancel the appointment in advance, but you should never simply fail to follow through. Your interviewees are giving you their time. Treat that like the gift it is.

SAY "THANK YOU" IN TWO WAYS. This typically means saying "thank you" in your phone conversation and then following up with an email or "thank you" card.

NEVER ASK FOR A JOB. It is okay to let the interviewee know that you are looking for a job, but it is not okay to ask them to hire you. This is true in almost all cases, though there may be some exceptions. If your interviewee mentions an open position, it is completely acceptable to ask about the best way to apply for the position or what experience is required for the position.

NEVER ASK ABOUT THE INTERVIEWEE'S CURRENT SALARY. While I am generally in favor of asking direct questions, this is one that may catch your interviewee off guard and may be considered rude. Given this, it is okay to ask for general salary ranges for positions of varying seniority in this career path.